Library of Congress
Cataloging-in-Publication Data
Hart, Avery.
    Kids make music! : clapping and tapping from
Bach to rock / Avery Hart and Paul Mantell.
p.   cm.
"A Williamson kids can book."
Includes index.
Summary: Presents a variety of activities based on
music including singing and dancing, improvisation,
and making homemade instruments.
ISBN 0-913589-69-1
1. Games with music.   2. Musico-callisthenics.
[1. Music.   2. Games with music.]   I. Mantell, Paul.
II. Title.
MT948.H28   1993
780—dc20   93-2007
                                                     CIP
                                              AC MN

Cover & interior design: Trezzo-Braren Studio
Illustrations: Loretta Trezzo-Braren
Printing: Capital City Press

Williamson Publishing Co.
P.O. Box 185
Charlotte, Vermont 05445
1-800-234-8791

Manufactured in the United States of America

10 9 8 7 6 5 4 3 2 1

Paul Mantell and Avery Hart are the authors of
numerous other books including Williamson
Publishing's *Kids & Weekends: Creative Ways to Make
Special Days.*

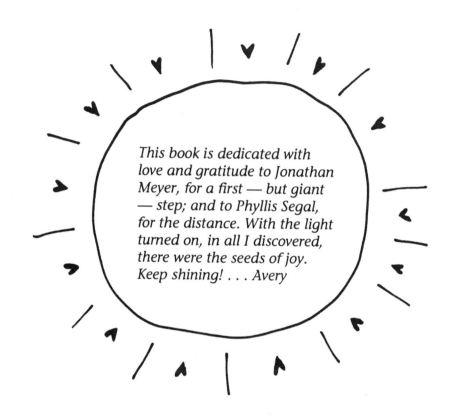

This book is dedicated with
love and gratitude to Jonathan
Meyer, for a first — but giant
— step; and to Phyllis Segal,
for the distance. With the light
turned on, in all I discovered,
there were the seeds of joy.
Keep shining! . . . Avery

KIDS MAKE MUSIC!

Clapping & Tapping from Bach to Rock!

AVERY HART & PAUL MANTELL

Illustrated by Loretta Trezzo Braren

WILLIAMSON PUBLISHING CHARLOTTE, VERMONT 05445

PROGRAM

Our deep thanks and appreciation to Susan Williamson, for her outstanding editorial inspiration and personal warmth; to E.L. Doctorow for his unique and magical approach to creative writing; to Susan Cohen and Writer's House, for making this book possible; to Barry Berg for his warm and intelligent support; to Liza DiSavino, Cathleen Bullivant, Elliott Raines, and Katherine Hannauer for their musical expertise, and Louis D'Amico for the drum cadences.

Thanks also to Steve Blucher, Amanda George, Andrew Howard, Ray Leslee, and Tom Colao and the New World Quintet for their musical inspiration; to Victoria La Fortune for her rare friendship and positive support in all our endeavors; to Maria Avitable for her long-standing belief in both of us; to Linda Halper, for her sensitive caring and practical support, Jeremy Halper for the inspiration of "Living Room Lounge," and Rob and Zachary Halper for their friendship and love of music; to the ageless and ever-dancing Abe and Vivian Halprin, and Mildred and Jack MacGeachie; to Fran Rogers, and Amina Jannah for dance expertise; to Jyoti Chrystal and Jason Martin for the fire; to Adele Getty for the Great Spirit chant.

Last on the list, but first in our hearts, thanks to our sons Matthew Mantell, for his many creative and practical suggestions for this book, and Clayton Mantell for his on-going inspiration in all we do. Thanks also to our parents, Irene Brino Wagner and Sol and Millie Mantell, for their enduring belief in our abilities and practical support during the writing of this book.

Paul Mantell and Avery Hart

OVERTURE

EVERYONE'S A MUSIC MAKER

There's something magical in people — something that comes out whenever we sing, clap, or sway to a beat. It shakes out through our shoulders and hips. It blows out of our lips, and it shivers out our shoulders. It gets out however we can get it out.

We're talking about music, of course. And one thing is for sure — music is downright necessary! Without it, we wither. So it doesn't matter how young — or old — we are, or if we sing like a bird or a buffalo. It doesn't matter if we can play an instrument, or just play ball. We still need music. We need it to clean out our feelings, and move us. We need it to express what words alone can't say. We need the magic carpet ride it takes us on. We need it to keep us "all the way 'live."

That's why *Kids Make Music!* is designed to get you up and humming, clapping, singing, whooping, and drumming. Just for the fun of it. Because music is necessary.

You won't need any special training or equipment to explore this book, either. If your heart is beating, you already have everything you need to make music.

So get ready to explore your great musical insides! "Thar's gold in them hills," and there's music in you. Yes, it really is there, waiting for you to shed your shyness and unlock the door marked "feelings." Soon, you'll be playing it straight from the heart — the place that music really comes from. *Kids Make Music!* aims to get you off to a good start in your musical self-discovery.

THE MOST AMAZING INSTRUMENT

• THE ULTIMATE MUSIC-MAKING MACHINE •

It sings. It whistles. It stomps. It pulses. It claps. It makes up tunes. It spins and swirls. It hums. It's the most amazing instrument ever. It's you!

From the tip of your toes to the top of your head, your body is packed with musical powers just waiting to be discovered and let out. And just think, all you had to do to get this magical instrument was to be born!

Like every musical instrument, though, you've got to know what it does before you can play it. Even a million dollar violin is just an interesting piece of wood until someone picks it up and plays it. So get ready to take a tour of the merchandise, exploring the most amazing instrument ever — you!

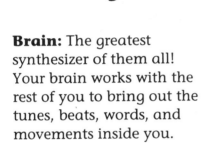

Brain: The greatest synthesizer of them all! Your brain works with the rest of you to bring out the tunes, beats, words, and movements inside you.

Eyes: Imagine; pick up cues

Ears: Pick up sounds to play along with

Mouth, lips, and tongue: Sing, click, whistle, squeak, and whoop

Voice box: Vibrates the sound you hum or sing

Fingers: Snap and pop and thump

Wrist: Pulse point

Arms: Wave or sway to the beat

Neck: Pulse point

Hands: Clap, slap, rap, and jive

Lungs: Give power to your sound

Heart: Best beat keeper in the world; place where your feelings live

Swiveling hips: Shake, rattle, and roll; add "oomph" to your music

Thighs: Clap like a big bass fiddle

Legs: Dance and leap

Knees: Knockers

Feet: Stomp, pound, and drum; happy feet for dancing

Toes: Tap out a beat

It's amazing, but true! The ultimate music-making machine is you!

• WHAT A TALENTED FACE! •

Cheek popping, lip bibbling, face drumming, wah-wahing — yes, you can do them all! You'll find out just how talented your face really is.

Cheek popping is an ancient art. To pop your cheeks, puff them out as far as they will go, with your mouth firmly shut. When your cheeks are fat and filled with air — you guessed it — pop them with the palms of your hands. The air inside your mouth will explode out, making a popping sound.

Another kind of pop can be made by putting the tip of your finger into your open mouth and popping the cheek. This takes some practice though. Some brilliant people can make a very big sound that way! Become a cheek popper and you'll have the perfect sound effect for *Pop! Goes the Weasel!*

Does *lip bibbling* sound like a silly thing to do? Well, it is. Very.

To bibble, hold your lips together loosely and flick your pointer finger up and down from nose to chin. We told you it was silly.

When you have a little experience, you'll be able to bibble whole songs by humming as you flick. Who knows, you may create a brand new sensation and get on TV!

Face drumming is a lot like cheek popping, before the pop. When your cheeks are big, tap them with your palms and you will hear a drum-like sound.

To *wah-wah* or *whoop*, open your mouth, and say "Ahhhhhhh" while quickly covering and uncovering your lips with the palm of your hand. Kind of sounds like an echo, doesn't it?

• CELEBRATE YOURSELF IN SOUND •

Your body is a musical instrument all ready to make music. How about making up a special song that uses all the sounds you can make?

I got feet, feet, feet, feet,

They're so neat, neat, neat, neat,

Listen to what my feet can do!

(Make sounds with your feet: slap them on the floor, tap your toes, pound your heels.)

I got hands, hands, hands, hands,

And they can clap, clap, clap, clap,

And they can slap, slap, slap, slap,

My fingers snap, snap, snap, snap,

Listen to my hands!

(Make sounds with your hands: slap your thighs, snap your fingers.)

I got a tongue that can click (Click tongue)

Cheeks that can pop! (Pop cheeks)

Face like a drum (Drum face)

I can wah-wah if I'm glum (Wah-wah)

Bibble 'til I'm done!

•

Yes, that's me, me, me, me!

I'm so free, free, free, free!

I can jump, I can shout,

I can turn myself about,

I can clap, I can slap,

I can stomp, I can romp,

And I'll do them all together now!

(Have a free for all! Stamp feet, clap hands, click tongue, lip bibble, making all the musical sounds you can think of!)

Oh, yeeeeeeeeah!

• THE INSIDE BEAT •

There's a drum inside your body and it's drumming all day, every day — even when you sleep! You can feel this drum in your neck, wrists, or chest as your heart pumps your blood all around your body. A doctor might call it your *pulse* — we call it the *inside beat*.

Practically all music is based on the inside beat. Fast music matches the fastest heartbeat, and slow music matches the slowest heartbeat. That's why marching music is brisk and peppy, while a lullaby is slow and soothing. The march is designed to get you up on your feet, moving. But the lullaby is designed to slow your heartbeat down so you can sleep.

What's your inside beat doing right now?

Listen to the inside beat

Find a quiet place, put your hand over your chest, and feel for your heartbeat. If you have a doctor's stethoscope, great! (You can find the same rhythmic pulse on your wrist or on the side of your neck, too.) When you find it, say it out loud, "Da-dum, da-dum, da-dum." Your inside beat means that your music machine is turned on and running, ready to make music!

Can you make up a tune to go with your heartbeat? We bet you can. (For more on beat, see page 24–28.)

Clock the beat

If you're sitting quietly now with this book, chances are your heart is going at a medium beat — not so fast and not so slow.

Find a clock and count how many beats your body makes in a minute.

Then, go outside and run around the house for ten minutes, or do a hundred jumping jacks. Your heart will start beating a lot faster! How much faster? Clock the beat and find out!

• LISTEN UP! WITH ALL SIX EARS! •

People who know a lot about ears say we have six of them! There's two that we hang our sunglasses on, called the *outer ears*, two in the *middle*, and two inside, called *inner ears*.

Imagine what elephants hear!

Your outer ear is like a seashell that catches sound and makes it louder. Cup your ears and listen. Does changing the shape of your outer ear change the way you hear? Imagine how well animals with big ears can hear!

A drum in your head? A canal?

There's a drum in your middle ear, called a *tympanum* (TIM-pan-um), or eardrum. It's a tiny piece of skin stretched tight (like a drum) over the canal in your head — the auditory canal, that is. When sounds enter your ear, the eardrum vibrates, sending the sound further in.

A tool chest? An electric seashell?

Behind your eardrum are the tiniest bones in your body, called the *hammer*, the *anvil*, and the *stirrup*. They look like miniature carpenter's tools, and send the sound to the *cochlea*, which looks like a seashell. There, it meets the electricity of your nerves and travels to the brain where the sound is given meaning. And this all happens in no time, as sound travels at 1,100 feet per second!

• LISTEN LIKE A FISH •

Water carries sound vibrations differently than air. Next time you take a bath, put your ears under the water and listen to how water carries sound.

Experiment. Hold your hands above the water and "tickle" the surface. Hum an underwater tune. Scratch the sides of the tub with your fingernails.

Can you hear other sounds in the house, like a door closing or people walking? Do soft noises sound louder under water?

Imagine being a fish. Now you know how they "hear" all the time!

Noise alert — cover them up!

Some people think that music gets better the louder it is. The truth is, listening to loud music can damage your hearing. So if someone tells you music is best when it's blasting, run! Don't let a wrong idea hurt your ears.

THEY'RE PLAYING OUR SONG

WANT TO SEE A VIBRATION?

You can see the vibrations that make sound by putting a yardstick on a table and holding it down firmly with one hand. Swat the free end and you'll see the stick move rapidly, up and down. That's vibration!

Change the sound the vibration makes by changing the length of the stick on the table. When more of the stick is on the table, the free end makes short, fast vibrations and a higher sound.

When more is off the table, the vibrations will be longer, and make a lower sound.

Is it music? Or is it sound?

All music is sound. But not all sound is music. Take a few minutes to listen to whatever you can hear from where you are right now. Do you hear sound? Or do you hear music? Better yet, do you hear sound that could become music? For instance, a truck passing by may not

sound like music at first. But it could be the start of a song about trucks!

Have you ever been listening to your favorite music when a grown-up happens by and says, "How can you listen to that noise?" Well, part of the difference between sound and music is how you feel about it. If it's music to your ears, then, for sure, it is music!

• HOW TO WHISTLE •

Pucker up, music maker! Because the time has come to learn to whistle! Of course, you may already know how. If you do, go ahead and whistle right past this page.

But if you haven't learned to whistle yet, here's your chance! All you need for whistling is what you already have — one pair of lips, one set of lungs, and some patience.

Learning to whistle is kind of like riding a bike. You can't do it, you can't do it, you can't do it — then all of a sudden you're flying down the street.

Whistling in three easy steps

Step One: Shape your lips into a small "O."

Step Two: Place your tongue behind your lower front teeth.

Step Three: Take a deep breath and then let it out, tightening your lips around it as it goes.

No luck?

If the only sound that comes out is air, keep trying! We promise that if you keep practicing you'll soon hear a hint of a whistle. Before you know it, you'll be whistling all over town!

Whistling on both sides of your breath

Once you get the basic whistle down, you can learn to whistle on the in-breath as well as the out-breath. This will give you the ability to whistle whole songs without stopping to take air in. Now there's something to amaze your friends with!

A TOOTHBRUSH CONCERTO

Music can be part of your day, from morning 'til night. Even when you run up steps, or march around the house, you can do it musically. Tonight when you're brushing your teeth, try brushing them to a beat! You can pretend that you are a famous player who will be giving a *solo* performance — that means you'll be brushing alone as your audience listens.

You might want to have someone else do the singing on this one, so you don't swallow your toothbrush! Remember, practice makes perfect — and gives you a brighter smile, too!

VOICE:
Brushing, brushing, brushing,
Brushing to a beat!

SOLOIST:
Brush to the beat

VOICE:
Inside, outside,
Upside, downside,
Brush, and tap your feet!

SOLOIST:
Brush and tap

VOICE:
Right side, left side, all around,
Keep on with that brushing sound!

SOLOIST:
Brush solo

VOICE:
Don't stop yet, 'cause you're not done!
Till you've washed and brushed that tongue!
Soloist finishes up with an operatic gargle, and a dramatic — but well-aimed — spit into the sink!

VOICE AND SOLOIST:
Ta-da!

• HAND AND BODY JIVE •

Hand jive is music that's sung with your hands. In hand jive your hands make the motions that tell what the song is all about. In body jive — well, you guessed it!

Whoops Baby!

If you know a baby, she'll like this easy hand jive, and it will help introduce her to music, too. Count the first words on her fingers, starting with her pinky; then slide down the space between her forefinger and thumb on "whoops." When you reach her thumb, go back the other way.

Oh, baby, baby, baby, whoops, baby, whoops, baby, baby, baby, baby.

Cabin In The Woods

If you like wildlife, you'll like this hand jive song about a rabbit who is rescued from a hunter.

In a cabin (form a house with your hands)

In the woods (make your arm a tree stump with wiggling fingers as leaves in the tree)

A little man by the window stood (stand very straight)

Saw a rabbit (put your hand over your eyes)

Hopping by (use two fingers on each hand for a hopping motion)

Knocking at the door (pretend to knock on the door — stamp your foot for a sound effect)

Help me! Help me! The rabbit cried (hold up your hands and widen them helplessly)

Before the hunter shoots my hide! (pretend to shoot a rifle)

Come little rabbit, come inside (pretend to open the door)

Safe with me abide!* (pretend you are holding the rabbit close to your chest)

* abide is an old-fashioned word for "stay"

The ultimate hand and body jive

Shimmy Shimmy Cocoa Puff is one of the best hand jive songs around, and it includes the whole body. On the "shimmy, shimmy cocoa puff" part, let your bones slip and slide any way you want, but freeze on "pow!" For the motion of the head, tilt your head side to side toward your shoulders. Act out the other parts of the song with your hands and body, too.

Shimmy Shimmy Cocoa Puff

Down, down baby, down by the roller coaster (Roll your arms like a moving roller coaster tram)

Sweet, sweet baby, I'll never let you go

(Hug yourself as you sway from side to side)

Shimmy shimmy cocoa puff,

(Make it up!)

Shimmy shimmy pow!

Shimmy shimmy cocoa puff,

Shimmy shimmy pow!

Gramma, Gramma sick in bed (Put your hand to your forehead as if you have a headache)

Call the doctor, and the doctor said (Pretend to make a phone call)

Let's get the motion of the head — ding dong! (Tilt your head from side to side)

Let's get the motion of the hands — clap, clap!

Let's get the motion of the feet — stomp, stomp!

Put it all together and what do you get?

Ding dong! Clap clap! Stomp stomp!

Say it all again and what do you get?

Ding dong!

Clap clap!

Stomp stomp!

Say it all backward and what do you get?

Stomp, stomp!

Clap, clap!

Ding dong!

A MELODY, A FEELING, & A BEAT

All it takes

All the music in this whole wide world is made of just three things: a *melody*, a *feeling*, and a *beat*. Melody is the way the sounds of a song come one after another. Feeling is the emotion music carries. The beat is the pulse of the music.

When you get those three together, music *will* happen — absolutely, for sure, no doubt about it!

A *melody*, a *feeling* and a *beat* run in, under, over, and through every song ever written. They are in all the music you hear on tapes, the radio, TV, and at the movies.

Why? Because without them, music cannot happen. With them, music can't be stopped!

A MELODY

• TURN ON A TUNE •

A melody (or *tune*) is what you do after you say, "I know that song! It goes . . . ." It's the da-da-da-dee-dum, the la-la-la- lu-la, and the bibbity-bobbity boo.

Melodies are kind of like squiggly lines made from sound — they go up, they go down, they go all around.

Making up a tune is like drawing, with your voice as the crayon. You can make up millions of tunes just by letting yourself hum or da-da-dum freely

Try it now. Just hum — or la-la-la — a piece of a song you've never heard before. You see! When it comes to making up tunes, human beings are born brilliant!

• DRAW A MELODY •

Put on a slow song that you know, or ask someone to sing one slowly for you. As you listen, draw a line across the wide part of a piece of paper. When the music goes up, draw your line up. When it goes down, draw your line down. You can make your melody line in a spiral shape, too.

After you've made a few melody lines or spirals, put them away for a while. When you take them out again, can you guess the songs they were made from?

• SING THIS BOOK •

Here, and in other parts of this book, you'll find bunches of words without melodies to go with them. These words need melodies to save them from being too quiet on the page. The reason we couldn't write the melodies for these words is simple — the tunes for them are in *your* head! All you have to do is open up and let the melodies out!

What tune do you have in your head for these words?

You can't do it wrong

When you make up a song

Any tune you create

Will turn out sounding great!

Millions of right ways

There are *no wrong ways* to make up tunes. But there are *millions of right ways*!

Some people start making up tunes by *chanting* the words they want to set to music. Chanting is saying words out loud to a steady beat. After you chant a while, a funny thing happens. Suddenly your voice will want to go up or down, just for fun. When that happens, success! You're making a melody!

Some people start by *clapping* their hands to get a beat and a feeling going before they start making a melody up. That's a good way, too.

So is just plunging in, blurting it out — on the spot. That's called *improvisation*.

Surprise yourself

When you improvise a tune, you open up and sing — anything, any way! The music just flows out of you all by itself. All you have to do is stay out of the way, and let it happen! You'll be amazed at how much music is inside you when you do!

If you can borrow a tape recorder to catch your creations, great. But the really important thing is to throw yourself into the "improv" and have fun.

SET A POEM TO MUSIC

Poems are perfect for making up tunes because the words they're made from already have a beat. Speak, chant, or sing these words out loud, and we'll bet you discover a melody floating around in your head that's perfect for them. You can call your creation, *Starlight*, by You!

> *Starlight, star bright*
>
> *First star I see tonight*
>
> *I wish I may*
>
> *I wish I might*
>
> *Have the wish*
>
> *I wish tonight.*

If you want to, add to your song with a musical list of the things you wish for.

Sing me! Out loud, strong, and proud!

The words of a song are called *lyrics*. They are words that fit well with music, or special poems, designed to be sung. We wrote these lyrics about making up a song. Now you get to make up the tune for us. Good luck, partner!

Music is a Feeling

When you make up a song

You've got to feel your way

Ask yourself are you happy today

If you are, make a song that goes

La, la, la — I'm happy!

•

But if you're feeling sad

Or kind of blue today

Don't resist, cause it's okay

Sing boo-hoo, and let a sad song

Come out of you, you, you!

•

Music is a feeling

That's what we mean to say

So if you want to shout

Just let that shout come out

And let the music plaaaaaay!

•

And however you feel

There is a song in you

And if it's from your heart

Then the song is true.

•

So sing for me

And I'll sing for you

Let's sing

La, la, la (you got it!)

Keep singing

La, la, la, la, laaaa!

• REMEMBERING THE TUNES YOU CREATE •

Writing or drawing the melodies you create will help you to remember them. Your notes have to show just two things:

1. Whether the notes go up or down.

2. If they are long or short.

Here are a few different ways kids have invented to write music down. They were writing the first part of *The Star Spangled Banner*. Look them over to see how they work, and then write down a melody line of your own. Borrow these methods, or make up a new one.

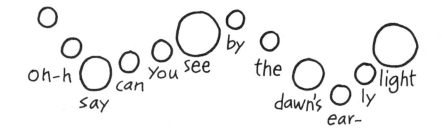

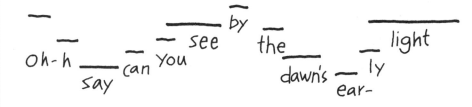

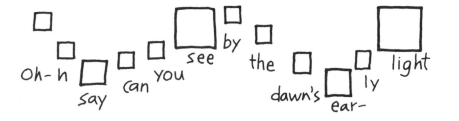

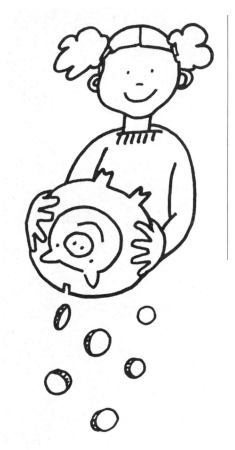

Money music

Here's a unique way to "write" music — with money! Make pennies stand for short sounds, nickels for longer sounds, and dimes for even longer sounds. Place the money higher or lower to show how notes go up or down.

This method of writing tunes is fun, but it can get expensive!

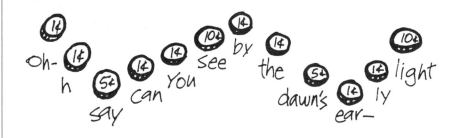

A FEELING

• FOLLOW YOUR FEELINGS •

Feelings take sound and spin it into pure music magic. Feelings are the fuel that make all music move. Feelings fire music up and make it fly. Music without any feelings would sort of be like life without colors, or food without taste. Pretty dull, huh?

Play the GLAD-SAD-MAD Two Hat Game

Want to have some fun with your feelings? All it takes is paper and a pencil, two hats, and a few tunes that everyone knows.

To get set up, find the hats. Then, write the words GLAD, SAD, and MAD on separate slips of paper. Fold up the slips and put them in one of the hats.

Next, write the names of some songs that you and your friends all know — songs like *I've Been Working on the Railroad, Three Blind Mice, Twinkle, Twinkle, Little Star*, or any other song you know. Fold up the song titles and put them in the other hat.

Each player chooses a slip from each hat, so that they get a feeling and a song. Now the fun begins!

Take turns singing out the song you picked with the feeling you picked behind it. See if the other players can guess the emotion you're trying to show.

When you play this game, don't be afraid to ham it up! The bigger your expression, the better.

• AN EMOTIONAL ALPHABET •

Expert SAD-GLAD-MAD Two Hat players can use this emotional alphabet to find different feelings from 'A' to 'Z' to express. Just pick one out and try to express it in song. Or, tell your friends you're picking a 'B' or 'D' feeling, and let them try to guess which one.

Will you choose Able? Anxious? Amiable? Blue? Bouncy? Bashful? Blissful? Crying? Cold? Confident? Crummy? Delightful? Determined? Dull? Easy going? Envious? Frustrated? Frightened? Full of beans? Fuming? Generous? Great? Happy? Horrified? Innocent? Icky? Joyful? Jealous? Kindly? Loving? Lousy? Mean? Masterful? Mischievous? Nasty? Nervous? Nice? Open? Optimistic? Playful? Quiet? Quick? Raucous? Robust? Silly? Starry-eyed? Sensational? Tearful? Terrific? Unhappy? Victorious? Wonderful? X-static? Yukky? Zippy? Zany? — or something altogether different?

• ANTI-SCARE SONGS •

There's an old song that goes, "Whenever I feel afraid, I whistle a happy tune . . . ." By the end of the song, the person who is singing isn't afraid anymore!

You can tame your fears with music, too. If you are afraid of something, start humming and then make up a song about it. Chances are good that your song will chase your fear away. Songs have a way of doing that. Try it and see!

Sing this section. These words are waiting on the page for someone to make them into music. Just give them a feeling, a beat, and a made-up melody and you'll have created a song!

The Bedtime Monster Song

When it's dark at night

I am full of fright

There's a monster under my bed!

I called my mom, and that's what I said!

•

Mom came in to me

Got down on her knee

There's no monster anywhere here!

Just some junk and dusty underwear.

•

No monster? No monster?

Are you sure? Let me look!

Hey! Yippee! What do you know!

There's my missing library book!

•

Mom, please shut the light

Tuck me in real tight

Off to dreamland I am gonna zoooooom!

There's no monster here!

And anything is better than cleaning up my room!

•

Good night!

Boom-chicka-boom-chicka-boom-chicka-boom

When a music maker starts a song by saying, "And a one, and a two, and a . . ," what he's doing is setting up the beat. The beat is the pulse of music, the way your heartbeat is the pulse of your body. It's how time is counted in music. Another word for beat is *rhythm* (RIH-thum).

You make up a beat by clapping or tapping one sound after another.

The beat of a song is kind of like the ground that a flower will grow in. The ground has to be there before the flower can grow. In music making, the beat is the ground your song will grow in.

THE BEAT'S IN THE BOX

If you have an empty carton and a wooden spoon, then you have a way to drum the basic beats that most music is made from.

Here's how it works:

Use the spoon to hit the inside of the box, one side at a time. Then keep hitting them in the same order. The **1-2-3-4** beat you'll create is a very common beat — so common that it's called *common* time! There are about a zillion songs written in this time, like *This Old Man*, *America the Beautiful*, and *We Shall Overcome*.

One, two! One, two, three!

This time, try striking just two sides of the box, **1-2**. The 1-2 beat is under lots of songs, too — usually quick ones like *Oh Susannah* and *John Henry*.

If you strike three sides of the box, you'll hear a **1-2-3** beat, which is also called *waltz time*, after a graceful, old-fashioned dance. Try it and listen for the beat behind *Take Me Out to the Ball Game, Rock-a-Bye Baby* and *On Top of Old Smokey*, plus oodles of other songs.

Your carton is like a drum machine that can help you keep the beat! What talent!

BEATS IN THE BOX
(X marks The place you strike)

Basic 4/4 BEAT
(1-2-3-4)

X1   2X
X4   X3

Basic 1-2 BEAT
X1
X2

Waltz BEAT
(1-2-3)
X1   2X
X3

THE MUSICAL CLOCK

On the clock, there are seconds, minutes, hours, and days. In music, it's beats, measures, phrases, and songs!

Be a grandfather clock

You may be a kid now, but if you have a tape measure that pulls out and springs back, you can become an instant grandparent! Well, a grandfather clock anyway. These old-fashioned time pieces have pendulums in them that swing back and forth to mark the seconds.

Let the tape measure be your pendulum. It will swing more quickly or more slowly, depending on how long you make the tape. A short tape will make a quicker beat, or *tempo*. A longer tape makes for a slower tempo.

The grandfather clock game

Here's a funny game to play. One person is the tempo keeper. The tempo keeper swings his grandfather pendulum while the other person hums or sings a simple song with an easy rhythm, like *America the Beautiful*. During the song, the singer starts to go faster and faster as the clock tries to keep up. Then, the singer goes slower and slower, trying to sing as slowly as possible. This game creates a lot of giggles.

• MAKE A CLAP BAND •

All you need are sets of hands and you can make a rhythm band! To start, choose one person to start off the rhythm. At first the band will clap out whatever he claps. This will warm up the band and get everyone working together.

```
Leader:     X X X X X X X X X X X X X X X X
Followers: X X X X X X X X X X X X X X X X
Leader:     X X X X X X X X X X X X
Followers: X X X X X X X X X X X X
Leader:     XX X XX X XX X XX X
Followers: XX X XX X XX X XX X
```

Now that you know your clap band can work well together, try making up new rhythms by giving different claps extra oomph!

Here's an example:

```
Clapper #1:   X X X X X X X X X X X X
Clapper #2:   X X X X X X X X X X X X
Clapper #3:   X X X X X X X X X X X X
```

Use homemade drums to play out the rhythms, too (see *Musical Toys*, page 60). How long can you play? How fancy can you make the rhythms?

Stop, Look, and Listen!

Are you ready to get your mojo (internal energy spirit) working? Are you ready to throw yourself into a beat? This beat game gets your whole body moving!

To play, make your feet into two big drums and start stamping a strong 1-2 beat with them. When you've got a strong beat, keep it going! Then clap out every syllable of these words with your hands (the word stop equals one syllable, before equals two syllables):

Stop, look, and listen

Before you cross the street!

Always use your eyes and ears

Before you use your feet!

Who's Got the Beat?

"Who's Got the Beat" is a great game to play with a friend or two. It's a lot like "Stop, Look, and Listen," but in this game, you try to guess the song being clapped. To start, think of a song that you and your friends are sure to know, like *Jingle Bells*. Then give your friend a clue about the song, for instance, "It's a winter song."

Begin stamping out the basic beat (4/4 or common time), and add the rhythm of the words in claps (without singing). See if your friend can guess the song you're clapping. If she can, let her choose the next song to stamp.

Take Me Out to the Ball Game

Here's a clapping game to play when you sing this famous song:

Motion #1: Slap palms with a partner, or if you're by yourself, raise your arms, as if rooting for the team.
Motion #2: Clap hands.
Motion #3: Slap your thighs.

Begin by getting a steady 1, 2, 3 beat.

1,2 3 1   2 3 1,2,3 1,2,3
Take me out to the ball   game

1,2 3 1   2 3 1,2,3, 1,2,3
Take me out to the crowd

1   2   3   1   2   3   1,2,3 1,2,3,
Buy me some peanuts and crackerjacks

1,2 3   1   2 3 1 2   3   1
I   don't care if I never come back

2   3   1,2 3   1   2   3   1,2,3, 1,2
For it's root, root root for the home team

3 1,2 3   1   2   3 1,2,3,1
If they don't win it's a shame!

2,   3   1,2,3   1,2,3 1   2   3   1
Cause it's one,   two,   three strikes, you're out!

2 3 1,2,3   1,2,3 1,2,3, 1!
At the old   ball   game!

(Once you've learned this game, try reversing the movements in the middle of the song for an extra challenge.)

The Beat Boss

Here's a rhythm game to try if you've got a few friends handy. Everyone — except "It" — sits in a circle. "It" leaves the room, and the others choose a "Beat Boss." The Beat Boss starts a rhythm with her hands, feet, or any other part of her body, and everyone else imitates her. Once the beat gets going, "It" comes back into the room.

Now comes the fun part. Every so often, the Beat Boss must change her body movement — but not the beat — without letting "It" see. The others in the circle pick up the new movement and try to mimic it perfectly.

"It" studies the kids in the circle, and tries to guess who is the Beat Boss. If he's right, he gets to choose the next Beat Boss. If he's wrong, he has to be "It" again.

HUNT DOWN SOME RHYTHMS

Wise people say that everything in the world has a rhythm all its own, even quiet things. You can find out if it's true by hunting for the rhythms in the world around you.

Go to a place where you can see people walking, working, or moving around. Does each person seem to have his or her own special rhythm? Tap the rhythm out, or sway your shoulders to the beat. That will bring those hidden beats to life.

Hunting rhythms at home

How many beats are going on in your house right now? Here's a fun "explore" that requires a little traveling to try to find the rhythms in your house.

If your brother is playing ping-pong in the basement, you'll find a strong beat there. But how about Grandma working her knitting needles in the family room? Any rhythm there?

Check out Dad chopping vegetables in the kitchen. Or, Mom raking leaves in the yard. How about the

dog's tail wagging? Or, your baby brother snoring? Find any rhythms?

Try listening for the beat everywhere in your house, from the basement to the attic. Pay special attention to the appliances in your house. The whir of the clothes washer and the beep of the microwave have their own rhythm, too — if you listen for them.

TEMPO!

Let's talk *tempo* (TEMP-oh)! How fast is a beat? How slow? That's tempo. But whether it's quick or slow, the basic rule for tempo is, it's got to be steady.

Play How Fast? How Slow?

To play this game, you sing a song — any simple song you know, like *Hickory Dickory Dock* — three times in a row.

The first time you sing it, clap your hands to the beat, and sing it as you have heard it before, at a regular rhythm. The second time, sing it as slooo-oow as you can, as you clap out a slow beat.

The third time, make it as fast as you can! But remember to keep the beat steady!

Try speeding up and slowing down other songs. If you're playing with friends, see who can go fastest and who can go slowest without losing the beat. (And if you start to giggle, remember, giggling has its own tempo.)

This is fun to do with "Stop, Look, and Listen," too.

LISTEN FOR THE MAGIC THREE

It's fun to pick out the magic three ingredients of music. Just turn on some music and try to find each one. Of course, you'll hear all three elements at once. But for fun, try to pick them out one at a time. Listen for the melody — the way the sounds lead from one to another. Then ask yourself, "What *feeling* did the music maker have when she made up this music?" How about the beat of the music? Tap it out as you discover it.

When you discover the feeling, the melody, and the beat, you will be discovering the body, the heart, and the soul of music!

A tune, an emotion, and a rhythm?

You can call a *melody*, a *feeling*, and a *beat* by different names, if you want. You could say that music comes from a *tune*, an *emotion*, and a *rhythm*. But that's just using different words to say the same thing. No matter what you call them, a *melody*, a *feeling*, and a *beat* are still, and always will be, the three magical ingredients of all music.

GOTTA SING!

A singing superstar — YOU!

Stand tall. Stand proud. Open up, and sing out loud! That's all there really is to singing. Just the doing of it. All it takes are two strong lungs, a throat, and a mouth to open up and let your song out!

Take a stand

To get the most sound out when you're singing, plant your feet firmly on the ground, and hold your head high. Then, throw back your shoulders and relax. In this position, your lungs can expand to give you the greatest power.

If you don't believe us, try this experiment. Round your back, hunch your shoulders, cave your chest in, and tuck your chin onto it. Now, try to sing. It's kind of hard to get sound out that way, isn't it?

But if you straighten up and widen your shoulders, hold your head up proudly, and open your mouth wide when you sing — watch out! The sound that will come out will be packed with singing power!

Breathe deeply

Singing takes a lungful of air. Put your hands, fingertips touching, on top of your stomach. Now, take a deep breath. Your fingers should move apart, not out, as your lungs widen.

Special message for people who think they can't sing

Okay, listen up, because here comes the plain and simple truth: *Everyone can sing, even people who think they can't.* Why? Because just as everyone has a one-of-a kind face, we all have a one-of-a-kind voice. Some voices are smooth and silky, some are rough and gravelly, some are strong, and some are gentle. But every voice has singing power — even yours.

Think about this: Some of the world's most famous singers — like Rod Stewart, or Rolling Stone Mick Jagger — have voices that are kind of ordinary. What makes their singing super is the feeling and energy they put into their music. That's what will make your singing special, too.

Sing this

Oh, I can sing everywhere!

On the stairs! In my room!

I let it ring! I let it zoom!

I sing it soft! I sing it loud!

I sing it strong! I sing it proud!

And wherever, wherever, wherever I am

Whenever, whenever, whenever I can

I open up, I open up and sing —

Yes, I can sing, sing, sing, sing

I can sing — everything!

A LITTLE BOX WITH BIG POWER

The reason that singing is simple is the musical dynamo located right in the middle of your throat — your voice box. When you sing, your voice box vibrates the sound, making the sound bigger and bigger.

Talk about musical power! Your voice can go up or down, fast or slow, soft or loud. (How loud? Just ask a grown-up about when you were a baby.)

Feel your voice box

Put your hand on your throat and hum. (Humming is singing with your mouth closed.) The vibrations you'll feel come from your voice box. With your hands on your throat, hum up, and then down. Does the vibration seem to go up and down in your throat, too?

• A SINGING PLAYGROUND •

Exploring your voice is fun when you pretend that it's a playground. Just think of the big toys in your local park. Then ask yourself, how would they translate into singing?

Go on the slide

If you like to climb the slide in the playground, pretend that your voice is the slide. Begin at the bottom, and start climbing up the slide steps, clump, clump, clump, until you reach the top. Then sliiiiiiiiide down, by singing, "Ahhhhhh!" from the top of your voice to the bottom.

You can make your singing slide straight or twisting. When you get to the bottom, end with a bump!

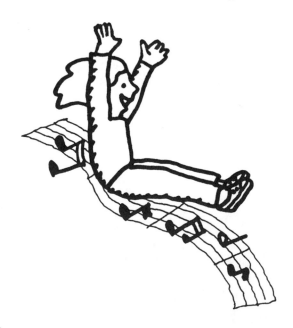

A musical see-saw

Sing a see-saw with a friend, because this game takes two voices. One person starts on a high note — as high as he can make it — while the other person starts way down low. Then, looking in each others eyes, they see-saw. The high one goes down and the low one comes up! When the players are balanced in the middle, they'll be singing the same note.

Sing a swing

Pretend your voice is a swing that starts slow and rises higher, back and forth, back and forth, higher and higher to touch the sky.

Musical catch

Playing musical catch is a lot like playing catch with a ball, except in this game the ball you toss is a tune. For example, one person sings, "Oh, I come from Alabama with a banjo on my knee, and I'm bound for . . . ." When he feels like it, he tosses the "ball" by throwing the melody to another player. If the other player is alert, she'll pick up the tune without missing a beat: ". . . Louisiana, my true love for to see." If the beat is missed, start the song again. Play for points or play for fun.

Give yourself a gift

When you learn the words of a song you like, you give yourself the power to sing that song whenever you want. Good for you! Because a song is a terrific gift to give to yourself! And just think, even if you give the song to someone else, by singing it for them, you'll still have the gift to keep for yourself!

• SING ON THE VOWELS •

One of the secrets professional singers use to make their singing better is *singing on the vowels* and passing by consonants as quickly as they can. That's because vowels are sounds made with the throat loose and open, allowing more sound to come out. Consonants stop sounds. Vowels echo sound.

Vowels: A E I O U (sometimes Y)
Consonants: B C D F G H J K L M N P Q R S T V W X Z

Speaking voice: *Home, home on the range*
Singing voice: *Hoooohm hoooohm aaaanhn th'raaaange*

Speaking voice: *Skip to my Lou*
Singing voice: *Skiiiip tooooo m'Looooo*

Speaking voice: *Who are you?*
Singing voice: *Whoooo aaahr yoooo?*

• SING YOUR NAME •

Even a name can be a song! It's a simple song to create — just sing your name out loud, over and over.

How many notes are in your name?

If your name is Jane Doe, or Joe Smith, it's two notes long. If your name is Jimmy Hill, or Ann Harris, it's a three-note name. As you can see, the number of notes is the same as the number of syllables in your name.

So, do you have a four-note name, like Nathan Friedman, or Jessica Jones? Or a five-note name, like Samantha Plummer? Or a six-note name, like Anthony Canelo? Some people have even more notes in their names, like Elizabeth Cappolini, or Alexander Makowsky!

Antidisestablishmentarianism Jones

Whatever your name is, it's a ready-made song, there for the singing! To get started, sing out your name, loud and clear, in a *monotone* (all the same sound without any highs or lows).

Now, sing your name again, but this time, make the notes go up or down. Try it using your middle name or nick-name, too. Sing your name over and over, soft and loud. Sing it slow and fast. Sing it jazzy and sing it straight. Soon, out of all the many ways there are to sing your name, you'll discover a way that feels just right.

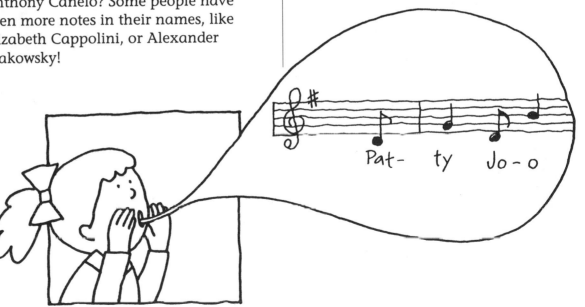

Pat- ty Jo- o

SING IN THE SHOWER

The bathroom is one of the best places for singing because the tile on the walls really makes sound ring! That's probably why so many people love to sing there!

If you've never sung in the shower or during a bath, you've been missing a lot of fun. But don't worry, as long as there's dirt, it's never too late to become a shower singer.

SING TO YOUR PET

Don't be surprised if your pet is one of your biggest fans when you sing! On the other hand, don't be insulted if he flattens his ears and skulks away whenever you burst into song. Animals react to music in all sorts of different ways.

Most animals seem to like music, though. We've even met one or two who seem to have favorite songs! If you're really lucky, your pet may even join in the fun, howling her head off!

• A MUSICAL GREEN THUMB •

Scientists have studied the effect of music on plants, and what they discovered is truly amazing! They found that corn actually grows better when classical music is played! Why not give it a try with your houseplants?

If you have two seedlings that are about the same size put them in different locations where they will get the same amount of light. Water and feed them the same, too. But sing to or play music for only one of them, and put the other in a place where it won't hear much music. You may be surprised to find that, after a time, the plant that has heard music is larger and healthier than the other one!

SING ALL YOUR FEELINGS — EVEN THE SAD ONES

We humans are lucky to have hearts that feel, because there's so much in life to feel good about. But when sad things happen, like a good friend moving away, those same hearts may feel like breaking.

Everybody in the world is sad sometimes. Yes, everybody. Sadness is an important part of being *human*. It may not be a fun feeling, but it's real, and it helps our lives to be real.

Singing lifts sad spirits

It may be hard to understand, but if you feel sad about something, that's good. It's good because you are experiencing a piece of your own, real, true life. But here's even better news. *Being* sad doesn't mean *staying* sad. Not when there's music in your life.

Music, being magic, can take a sad feeling and turn it around. Next time you're sad, put your feelings into music, and you'll see what we mean. If your hamster died, or if you miss someone, don't keep your feelings bottled up inside. Put on some music or make up a song for your sad feelings. Even if you only sing to yourself, singing will help free your sad feelings.

Song for a Loved Pet

I remember the feel of your fur

And the way that we played — together

How you'd run for the ball, tail wagging and all

Before you went to dog heaven

How you'd nuzzle your nose in my hand

And whenever I'd cry, you'd understand

You gave love in so many ways

Before you went to dog heaven

For a Lost Bird

Oh, yellow bird, oh bird, so sweet

My yellow bird, my parakeet

You didn't stay, you flew away

And I miss you so today

My yellow bird

I hope that you're safe in a tree

And that at last you're feeling free

Because wherever it was you flew

You took my heart and love with you

My yellow bird

LET'S HARMONIZE!

When sounds go together in a pleasing way, that's *harmony*. If there's a piano available somewhere, press a white note and a black note right next to it, together. Those notes don't sound good together; they don't harmonize.

Now play a white note plus another white note two above (leaving one in the middle). Don't they sound great together? That's because they harmonize.

Here's a way to discover harmony with a friend. Both people sing, "Do, re, mi" (pronounced "me"). (If you don't know what that sounds like, ask a grown-up.)

Now sing them again, but this time, one person holds the first note ("do" — pronounced "doe") and the other person holds the third note, "mi." The pleasant sound you hear when "do" and "mi" are sung together is harmony.

Discombobulating dissonance

Harmony is sounds that belong together. *Dissonance* is the opposite — it's sounds that clash.

Harmony is vanilla ice cream and hot fudge sauce. *Dissonance* is vanilla ice cream and gravy.

Harmony is mittens and scarves. *Dissonance* is sandals and snowsuit. Get it? Good!

Harmony

Dissonance

YOUR OWN BARBERSHOP QUARTET

Back in the old days when there were barbershops instead of hair salons, people started singing harmonies there, to pass the time away. The kind of music they created is called "barbershop singing," and it uses harmonies galore! The first *barbershop quartets* were usually made up of four men. There was a *tenor*, who sang high; a *second tenor*, below him; a *baritone*, with a medium voice; and a *bass* (pronounced "base"), who sang the lowest notes.

You don't need four people for barbershop singing, though. Two or more people — male or female — will do fine. One person will sing the main melody and the others will harmonize and echo the tune, creating the barbershop effect.

Some good songs for barbershop quartets are *By the Light of the Silvery Moon, Sweet Adeline, Down By the Old Mill Stream*, and *Down By the Bay*.

• THE BARBERSHOP LOOK •

Barbershop singing is so much fun that you may want to put on a concert for your family and friends. You can add to the fun by dressing up as if you were customers in an old-time barbershop. If you have long-sleeved white shirts, put them on, with a dark armband around the top of one sleeve. Old-fashioned wire-rimmed glasses and bow ties are good here, and so are fake handlebar mustaches, with hair slicked down and parted in the middle. (Trace handlebar mustaches from cardboard.)

A barber pole

In the background, have an old-fashioned red and white striped barber pole. You can make the pole from posterboard taped to make a cylinder and painted with red and white spiral stripes. First, paint the whole tube white (if it needs it). When the white paint dries, add a bright red stripe spiraling around the tube.

Down by the Bay

Try this song for some terrific barbershop singing. One person sings the main melody, and the others try every possible concoction of notes that harmonize. Try going up if the melody goes down, or down if it goes up. Or sing on one low note, or a high one. Soon you'll discover your own harmonies.

Singer #1: *Down by the baaaaaaaay*
Singer #2 (echoes as #1 sings "bay"): *Down by the bay*
Singer #1: *Where the watermelons grooooooooow*
Singer #2 (echo as above): *Where the watermelons grow*
#1: *Back to my hoooooooome*
#2 (echo: *Back to my home)*
#1 & #2: *I dare not go-o-o*
(harmonize up, harmonize down, harmonize all over the place)
#1: *For if I do-o-o,*
#2 (echo: *For if I do)*
#1: *My mother will sa-a-ay,*
2 (echo: *My mother will say)*
Solo (take turns being the soloist): *Did you ever see a bee?*
Drinking lemon tea? *****
All harmonize: *Down by the bay!*

*Make up your own line — any crazy, rhymed question will do. How about, "Did you ever see a fly, break down and cry?" Or, "Did you ever ride a bike, while singing in a mike?" Or, how about this one: "Did you ever harmonize, wearing a disguise?"

Sweet Adeline

That Adeline must have been quite a girl, because the song with her name in it became the most famous barbershop song ever! Here are the words, all ready to be lifted off the page and sung! Remember, one person sings the main melody and the other(s) echo and harmonize. Have fun!

> *Sweet Adeline,*
> *My Adeline*
> *At night dear heart*
> *For you I pine*
>
> ❤
>
> *In all my dreams*
> *Your fair face beams*
> *You're the flower of my heart,*
> *Sweet Adeline!*

• DOO WOP SINGING •

"Doo wop 'n shoobie doo, doo wop 'n shoobie doo, doo wop 'n shoobie doo, whoa-oh-oh-oh-oooooohhh!"

Try reading those words out loud. We'll bet you can't do it without a musical mood coming over you! You see, *Doo Wop* singing has a way of doing that to people. Plain, ordinary people will break into song as soon as they hear those time-honored sounds. Doo Wop is positively contagious!

How it started

You won't find the "History of Doo Wop" in an encyclopedia, but as far as we know, it was born in Brooklyn, New York, sometime in the 1950s. On hot summer nights, teenagers would stand on street corners singing the "popular" songs of the day.

Since they didn't have instruments, the teens used their voices instead. "Doo Wop 'n Shoobie Doo" probably stood for the sounds of a piano and snare drum. Doo Wop sounded so good that it soon caught on.

How to Doo Wop

In Doo Wop, there's a lead singer, usually the high tenor or soprano, who sings the melody of the song. Backing up the lead singer are his or her friends, who provide harmony and rhythm. The kid with the deepest voice adds the bass. That person will sing the rhythm as if he were a bass violin, something like, "bum, bum, bum, wah diddy-bum, bum, bum, wah diddy."

Finger snapping is used in the fast songs, and so are other Doo Wop phrases, like "yip, yip, yip, yip, ram a lam a ding dong," and more. Crooning harmonies, like "oh whoa" and "woo-ooo," add flavor in the slow songs.

Two famous Doo Wop songs are *In the Still of the Night* and *Blue Moon*. Groups that used Doo Wop include *The Four Seasons*, *The Platters*, and *The Persuasions*. Have a grown-up call a radio station and ask them to play some for you. After you've listened to it, we bet you and your friends will want to discover the Doo Wop inside of you!

• SCAT SINGING •

If you've ever heard someone sing something like, "Boh wah diddy oh, boh wah diddy oh, scooby, scooby doo, shoo bye oh, shoo bye oh . . . ," then you've heard scat singing. In scat singing, you use your voice like an instrument, making up nonsense syllables to go with the tune you're letting out. Scat singing is a kind of jazz singing, and is it ever fun!

Ella Fitzgerald, King Pleasure, and Sarah Vaughn were some of the greatest scat singers of all time. Someone in your family may have some of their music to listen to, or you can find it at the library.

You can scat sing, too. All you have to do is find some instrumental (music with no words) jazz music to sing along with. Find the jazz station on your radio — it's probably there somewhere on the FM band, and sing along, scat-style. Or, start singing a song you like in the usual way, and when you get to the middle of it, open up and scat!

• ROUNDS •

A *round* is a song that harmonizes with itself. When you sing the song, someone joins in at the right place, and the melody starts going around and around and around!

Singing a round is a lot of fun. The tricky part is sticking to what you're singing, while your friends are singing something else.

Row, Row, Row Your Boat

This may be the most famous round ever. It's a round with three parts. The second singer begins as the first singer gets to "Gently down the stream," and the third singer begins the song as the first sings, "Merrily, merrily, merrily, merrily . . . ."

Here are some other famous rounds. If you aren't familiar with them, find someone who can teach them to you:

Frere Jacques (Are You Sleeping?)

Hey ho, Nobody Home

White Coral Bells

Down by the Station

Dona Nobis Pacem (Give Us Peace)

Oh, How Lovely Is the Evening

Kookaburra

MELODY MUSH & MELODY MERGE

If you've ever been listening to the radio when your sister came through the room humming a tune, and your dad turned on the TV, which was playing a movie theme, you know that too much music played at the same time makes musical mush! You probably wanted to cover your ears to get away from the conflicting sounds, and who could blame you?

But did you know that some special songs all go together in a magical way? We call it melody merge. In fact, you can even play six merging melodies at the same time and they would sound great! Don't believe us? Well, stick around. We'll prove it by showing you how.

MELODY MERGE

Here's a list of some songs you probably know:

Swing Low, Sweet Chariot

When the Saints Go Marching In

Goodnight, Ladies

Amazing Grace

She'll Be Coming 'Round the Mountain

The Crawdad Song ("You get a line, I'll get a pole, honey")

Each song has its own special melody, but there's a secret to these tunes. If you sing or hum them all at the same time, without words, they sound fantastic together! The reason for this is called *counterpoint*.

Here's how to play:

Each person picks a melody to sing, "la, la, la" style. The first person sings his melody alone while the others clap to the beat. He keeps on singing but the second time through another player joins in with another melody from the merge list. Then comes the third song and so on, until everyone is singing together! *Remember, you can't sing the words in melody merge, because if you do, the merge will sound like mush.*

The secret to melody merge is keeping the rhythm steady, and sticking to the melody of the song you're singing — no matter what you hear from the other players.

Can you think of other melodies that will add to the merge? There are lots!

More melody merges

Here's another group of songs that fit well together:

Are You Sleeping?

Down by the Station

White Coral Bells

Row, Row, Row Your Boat

Three Blind Mice

Merrily We Roll Along

P. S. Melody merge works great with kazoos, too.

• EVERYBODY RAP! •

Yo, READer, READer, of this BOOK!

You wanna RAP right now?

You wanna TAKE a look

At a rappin kind of sound

And what it's ALL about?

It's gonna give you CLASS

It's gonna give you CLOUT

It's gonna get you tellin' stories from the INside OUT!

YO!

RAPper, RAPper, RAP with me

Let's get a REAL strong beat

As strong as IT can be

You can rap about your brother,

Or your sister, or your mother,

You can rap about your friend,

You can rap about your school

Hey, you can MAKE yourself

Into a RAPpin' fool!

And if you DO it right

It will be DYnomite

You'll be inTENsely cool

You'll start a RAPping school!

How cool? Like this, like this, like this,

Like this, like this, like this! How cool?

COOL JEWEL!

Yow!

Voice like a drum

Rap is singing like a drum. The word rap comes from *rapport*, which means a special, shared communication between people.

Rap music has a funky beat that stresses the off-beat which is called *syncopation*. This is rap:

> Come on and DANCE the DANCE
> The one you GOT from FRANCE . . .

This is not rap:

> You've GOT to DANCE
> The DANCE from FRANCE . . .

Make up a rap

You don't have to be a great poet to create rap. But you do have to be at least a little outrageous, and it also helps to have a great sense of humor. In rap, you can let your feelings fly — even your angry feelings. How about making up a rap that expresses your true and honest feelings about the extra homework your teacher laid on you last Friday? Hmm?

Another way to make up a rap is to take an event — imaginary or real, it doesn't matter — and put it into song. Like, "I was WALKing down the street, rapping to the BEAT, when my MOM came by and hit me with a PIE, I said, HEY my mom, what you DO that for? She said, listen UP, KID, I got a hundred pies MORE and I'm gonna smack 'em to you if you don't shut the DOOR when you LEAVE the house, not that I mean to GROUSE, but it's COLD outside and the heat bill's HIGH! This rap is ALmost done." Now you give RAP a TRY!

If you want to hear some great rap artists at work, look for music by the "Fat Boys," or "Naughty By Nature." Try out some Moonwalking and Hip Hop, too. Those are dances that go with rap music (see, *Gotta Dance!*, page 56).

• FAIRY-TALE OPERA •

You can be an opera star

An opera is a story told with music and song. Opera has some of the most passionate stories and music the world has ever known. If you like to act and sing, you can make up an opera with your family or friends. The story of your opera can be silly or serious. You can make up the story, or use one you already know. One way to start is by using a well-known fairy tale. Since you already know the plot, or story, of your opera, all you'll have to do is make up the music and act it out. Try it — it's fun!

RED RIDING HOOD, THE OPERA

If you have four people or more, you can perform a *Red Riding Hood Opera*. Some roles can double up. For instance, Red Riding Hood's mother and grandmother can be played by the same person.

The characters

Little Red Riding Hood

Little Red Riding Hood's mother

The Sly and Wicked Wolf

Grandma

The Woodcutter

Trees

If you have more people on hand, great! They can make a *chorus*. A chorus is a group of people who help tell the story of the opera. (If you don't have enough people for a chorus, the people playing the woodcutter and the grandmother can tell the story.)

Props and costumes

Props are objects that might be used during an opera. Little Red's basket and the woodcutter's axe are two important props, for instance.

As for costumes, Red should have a — what else? — a red hood! Grandma can have a shawl, one that the wolf will borrow when he's disguising himself.

Make an axe

You can make a wood-cutter's axe with cardboard and aluminum foil. Cut a long strip of cardboard, about 18" by 6". Double it the long way and staple it closed. Cut an axe head and cover it with foil. Staple it to the axe handle.

Red's Basket

Woodcutter's Axe

Grandma's Shawl

Red's Hood

What about the melody?

Make up the melody to your opera as you go along. You can't lose, if you remember to make the notes go up and down, and if you sing out whatever you are saying very clearly. Don't be afraid to ham it up, either! Opera is high drama, and anything goes — as long as it's outrageous!

Little Red Riding Hood — The Opera

Woodcutter character steps forward and announces (in made up song, of course): "Today, you lucky people, we present the story of Little Red Riding Hood! This enchanting tale, we hope you'll savor. It begins when Little Red's mother asks her for a favor!"

Enter Red Riding Hood's mother, holding a basket. She sings (something like this): "Red Riding Hood, come here! I've something for you, dear! It's a basket for your grandmother who lives in the deep, dark woods."

Enter Red Riding Hood, a cheerful girl, who takes the basket and answers her mother (in song, of course): "Give me the basket, Mom, and I'll bring it to Grandma."

Mother (sings, something like): "Fantastic, Little Red! But remember, do not stop to talk along the way! Grandmother is sick, and she needs that food today!"

To which *Little Red Riding Hood can sing out*: "Okay." (For an added effect, if you use these words, Mother can hold the "ay," from "today," and Red can harmonize with the same sound from her "okay.")

Red Riding Hood skips in a circle as the mother steps back, and out of the playing area. This will help the audience to understand that the location is changing. Red Riding Hood is now in the woods.

Trees (chorus) *sing*: "Here in the woods, we are the trees. Listen to mother, Red Riding Hood, please!"

The trees can shake their leaves (hands and fingers) and pretend that a harsh wind is blowing. *Trees sing*: "Wind . . . Oooohhhh! Aaaaahhh! Look who's here!"

Enter the Wicked Wolf. He or she should sneak onto the playing area as if unseen by Red. He sings (to the audience): "Ah, a little girl, what a treat! A nice, tasty bite for me to eat!"

Red Riding Hood sings: "Tra, la, la," or some other traveling music. Then she sees the Wolf, and her traveling music peters out. She looks afraid, but the wolf puts her fears to rest.

Wolf (singing cheerily): "Why, hello, little girl, good day, good day! Where might you be off to today?"

To which *Red sings*: "Oh, Mister Wolf, that I cannot say. Because I am not supposed to stray. I'm going to my grandmother's house in the woods today." (Hey, no one ever called Red brilliant, did they?)

Red Riding Hood skips off stage, weakly singing: Tra, la, la," and the *Wolf* skulks after her, perhaps with a wicked, and of course, musical: "Ha, ha, ha, ha, ha!"

Enter *Grandmother*, wearing a shawl. She sits in a chair, knitting. The next part of the story is told without words, just with musical screams and grunts. The chorus can comment with suspenseful moaning.

The wolf sneaks up on Grandma and locks her in an imaginary closet (out of the playing area). Once she is disposed of, he sits in her chair, knitting with the shawl around his shoulders.

Enter Red Riding Hood, who is very cheerful at first. She stops near the imaginary door of Grandma's cabin, and sings: "La, la, la! Hello, Grandma dear! Your little Red is here! I have some bread for you, and cheese and apples, too!"

Wolf (acting like Grandma, sings — repeating Red's melody will add to the effect): "Come in, child, and bring them close, my dear. My poor eyes are old, my vision isn't clear."

Perhaps the *trees* can sing out a warning here, from the side: "Little Red, stay away, or you will pay!"

But alas, *Red* moves closer to the wolf, then sings, in a low tone: "Oh, Grandmother. What big ears you have!"

Wolf sings: "All the better to hear you with, my dear."

Red steps toward Grandma (singing, perhaps a little higher): "Dear Grandmother, what big eyes you have!"

Wolf sings (same melody as his last line, but perhaps higher): "All the better to see you with, my dear."

Red sings: "Grandmother, what big teeth you have!"

Wolf sings (pulling out all the stops): "All the better to eat you with! Ha! Ha! ha!"

Wolf jumps up and attacks Red, who screams, musically, of course. (Opera singers never shriek — they *glissando*.)

Across the stage, a woodcutter is taking a whack at an imaginary tree. He hears Red's pitiful but melodious scream, and dashes to the center playing area.

Woodcutter (sings): "Hands off that girl! Let her free!"

Wolf (sings): "Why hello, Mr. Woodcutter, what do you know! Would you believe, I was just about to go! Toodle-oo!" He exits.

Backstage, someone stamps a foot hard. *Grandmother* sings with her hand over her mouth: "Let me out, let me out!"

The Woodcutter and Red find Grandma and free her.

Red sings: "Grandmother, dear!"

Grandma sings: "Thank goodness you're both here! Would you like some food?"

Woodcutter sings: "Oh, yes I would!"

Trees and Red sing: "It ended good!"

All: "Tra, la, la, la, la! Ha, ha, ha, ha, ha!"

This way of making up a *Red Riding Hood Opera* is just a suggestion, of course. The fun of making up an opera is choosing your own dramatic, silly, funny, or serious lines to sing.

SETTING THE TABLE: AN OPERETTA IN ONE CLASS ACT

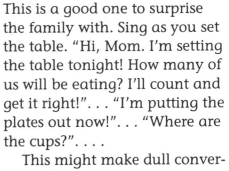

This is a good one to surprise the family with. Sing as you set the table. "Hi, Mom. I'm setting the table tonight! How many of us will be eating? I'll count and get it right!". . . "I'm putting the plates out now!". . . "Where are the cups?". . . .

This might make dull conversation, but when you sing it, even setting the table is fun.

Other operetta scenarios:

First day back-to-school

Vacation follies

The big ball game

When Grandma met Grandpa

Dreams of what I want to be

Camping in the wilderness

Don't want to stop singing? Check out *Sharing the Fun*, page 124.

GOTTA DANCE!

MOVIN' AND GROOVIN'

Dance is what happens when you're moving to the music, grooving to the beat. It's a way of saying, "Hey! I'm alive!" And not just saying it with words, but with your whole body!

Dance can happen from music that's inside your head, or it can happen when you hear music that lifts you up onto your feet, just for fun. When you dance, your body can stretch and wiggle, leap and prance. You can jump, slide, go, and flow. No wonder dancing feels so good!

• THE DINOSAUR DANCE •

Put on some fun music, or make up the melody, and do this dance!

If you want to be a dinosaur, here's your chance!

Just jump on your feet for a dinosaur dance!

Then plod on the earth at a lazy pace

And bare your teeth for a dinosaur face

•

Ohhhh, ohhhh, doing the dinosaur dance!

Thud, thud, doing the dinosaur dance!

Wave your arms like a big reptile

And do the dinosaur dance a while!

•

Ohhhh, ohhhh, doing the dinosaur dance!

Thud, thud, doing the dinosaur dance!

• FREE-FORM DANCING •

Free-form dancing is dancing just because you feel like it, any way you want. There are no rules and no steps to follow. It's just pure you, moving to music. You can stretch up on your tip toes, or plod around with your feet. You can wave your arms over your head and take giant steps, or you can sway to the music, practically standing still. Let the music tell your body what to do, and your dance will happen all by itself.

Scarf and streamer dancing

You can add to the fun of free-form dancing by carrying a scarf or streamer when you dance. The scarf or streamer becomes an extension of yourself — as if your arms grew to be five feet long. Suddenly, you and the music fill a big space! That's a good feeling.

Scarf and streamer dancing is a lot of fun when you play modern, classical, or any kind of music. Try it to Stravinsky's *Firebird* for a super-special experience.

Dance to a poem

Try this easy action dance. Someone reads (or sings) the poem while the others act it out. You can make up a melody to match the words as you read, too, if you want. But you may find that it's fun to dance to the rhythm of the words. That's right, poems are written in a rhythm called *meter*, and you can dance to their natural beat.

Can you walk on tiptoe

As softly as a cat?

And can you stomp along the road

Stomp like that?

Can you take some great big strides

The way a giant can?

Or walk along so slowly

Like a poor bent old man?

CREATE A BALLET

Ballet (ba-LAY) is a kind of dance that tells a story. What opera is to singing, ballet is to dance. Ballet is called classical dance because it follows strict rules and is usually performed to classical music.

Female ballet dancers are called *ballerinas*. They are muscular, strong, and sure on their feet, but they wear clothes that make them look light and delicate — almost fragile. They wear filmy short skirts called *tutus*, over *leotards* (top), and *tights* (bottom). Sometimes ballerinas wear special slippers, called *toe shoes*. Toe shoes have wood in them so that the dancers can dance up on their toes. Male ballet dancers are very strong and muscular, too. They wear leotards and tights, and sometimes have sashes on their waists. They often can jump or *leap* very, very high in the air.

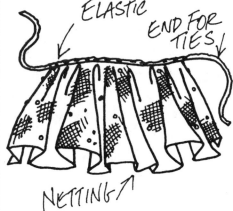

ELASTIC

END FOR TIES

NETTING

A tutu or sash for you

Making a tutu isn't very difficult. It just takes a strip of netting, or filmy fabric, a piece of elastic, a few pins, a needle, and thread. Stretch the elastic and pin it onto the netting, making a waistband. (Make sure to leave enough elastic at the ends to tie later.) Sew it onto the netting and remove the pins. For extra sparkle, dab dots of glue onto the netting and sprinkle them with glitter.

To make a sash, tie a long, flowing scarf around your waist. Or, take a piece of fabric twice as long as your waist and sew it in half lengthwise, leaving the end open (right sides of fabric inside). Now, turn the fabric right side out, and sew up the open end. You might want to decorate your sash with glitter or weave two brightly colored sashes together for extra pizzazz.

RIGHT SIDES INSIDE

SEW ENDS TOGETHER

TURN RIGHT SIDES OUT

SEW BOTTOM EDGE

THE FIVE POSITIONS OF BALLET

Ballet dancing has five body positions that are known to dancers all over the world. They are the language of ballet and the first thing a young ballet student learns. You can learn them, too! *Stand very straight and tall, with your head held proudly.* Put some gentle piano music on in the background to get in the mood.

   Once you're in one of the five positions, try a plie (plee-AY). To plie, hold the position and then slowly bend your knees as deeply as you can, keeping your back straight. Then, come back up slowly.

In *First Position*, you hold your arms downward, hands pointing to each other, so you're making a graceful oval shape. First position feet are together, with heels touching, back to back, and toes pointed as far as they can go in opposite directions. Good. Now, breathe deeply and plie!

In *Second Position*, your arms extend straight out at your sides, up to and including graceful fingertips. Your feet slide apart, still pointing outward. And now, plie!

In *Third Position*, the feet come back together with the heel of one jutted up against the arch of the other. Your curved arms reach forward gracefully, as if you are making a large circle with them. Your back is nice and straight and tall. You look positively wonderful, so plie!

In *Fourth Position*, the foot that was tucked against the arch slides forward. One arm goes up over your head and the other stays forward. Now, plie! Wow, what a ballet dancer you make!

In the *Fifth Position*, both arms extend over the head, in a graceful oval shape. The feet come together with one front to back and the other back to front. (This is a tough position for feet to get into, so just do the best you can!) And, plie! Step! Run! Leap!

NATIVE AMERICAN DANCES: THE POWER OF THE CIRCLE

Native Americans use dancing and singing as a spiritual celebration of being alive. They dance and sing about every part of their lives, even their dreams. They believe that singing and dancing have magical powers in them, powers that help the music makers send their messages right up to the heavens, to the Great Spirit!

Most Native American dances are done in a circle. Circle dancing brings people together. When you dance in a circle, everyone is free to express him or herself, and yet, everyone is still dancing together. Use dancing bells and homemade drums for these dances (see *Musical Toys*, page 58). Or, dance to Native American music that you've borrowed from the library.

Begin by putting the front of your foot on the ground, in a tapping motion, and follow by putting the whole foot down as you change feet and move forward. Try these basic beats to begin:

1 2 3 4 **1** 2 3 4 **1** 2 3 4
or
1 2 3 **4** 1 2 3 **4** 1 2 3 **4**

Better yet, drum with a friend and combine these beats.

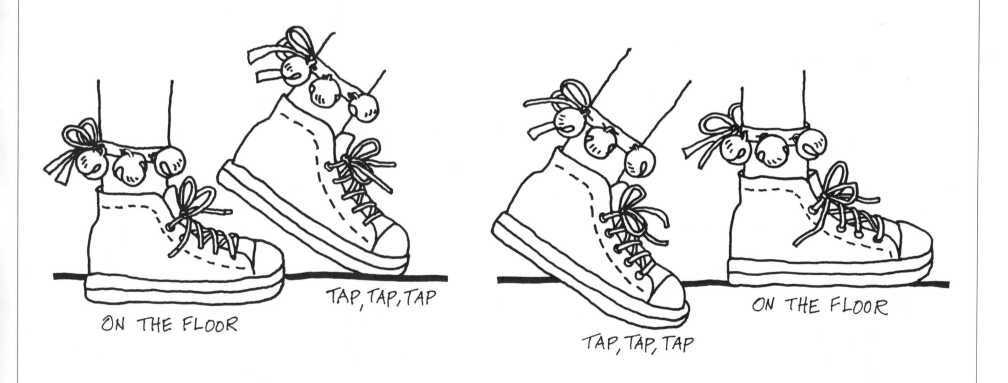

ON THE FLOOR   TAP, TAP, TAP

TAP, TAP, TAP   ON THE FLOOR

Your feet will set the rhythm of your dance, like a drum. Press your foot down firmly, really connecting to the Earth. Later, as the drumming rises, feel the drums and step any way you wish, even leaping and spinning, for as long as you want. You'll find yourself naturally returning to the basic pressing step. Maybe that's because the basic step symbolizes people's special connection to the Earth.

Dream dancing

Get a strong rhythm going on one of your homemade drums as you dance in a circle. Think about a good dream you've had. Pretend that you are having the dream all over again as you dance. Let your imagination add to the dream. Or, make up a whole new dream as you dance.

Plains Indian Sun Dance

The Oglala Sioux Native Americans celebrate nature in a *Sun Dance*, honoring the Great Spirit for creating the sun. Everyone in the community takes part in the Sun Dance, dancing out his or her personal thankfulness for the Sun's great powers.

You can do a sun dance, too, by doing what the Indians do. Celebrate the sun in a circle dance. Let your feet beat out a rhythm along with the drumbeat. When you dance, think about the sun, and all the ways it helps us to live. Think about its warmth, and the way it helps flowers and plants to grow. Imagine that warm sunshine is falling on your face and all over your body.

If you want, let your voice open up and tell about the power of *Wakan-Tanka*, who brings the sun. Chant your gratitude to Wakan-Tanka in words or sounds. Pretend you are the powerful sun yourself, shining your light and warmth all around.

If you get tired, quiet your motion down, but keep dancing. Part of the magic of the sun dance is the feeling you get when you dance for a long, long time. Try it and see.

• TAP DANCING •

Tap dancing is done with special shoes that have metal taps on the bottom of the toes and heels. That way every step you take clicks out a beat. It's as much fun to listen to tap dancing as it is to watch it!

You can tap dance, too, even if you don't have special shoes. Do it in two ways — by the *Happy Feet Method*, or by learning real tap dance steps.

Happy feet tap dancing

The Happy Feet Method of tap dancing is very simple. All you do is put on music with a quick 1-2 (or 1-2-3-4) beat and pretend to tap dance. Wave your arms around a lot as you slap your feet down and up in time to the music. Keep a giant-sized grin on your face as you let your feet fly!

Happy Feet Tap Dancing is so much fun to watch that you may even fool some people into thinking you really are tap dancing!

Real tap dancing

Okay, we admit it. Real tap dancing takes some practice. But what a pay off! Learning tap is like riding a bike — you never forget it once you learn. We have a friend who's much older than you who tap dances his boredom away whenever he has to wait for an important phone call.

Tap dancing doesn't take any skills you don't already have, either. If you break it down into its basic motions, you'll see how easy tap really is.

MAKE YOUR OWN TAP SHOES — OR TAP SNEAKERS

You can create tap shoes by putting coins on the soles and heels of old shoes — quarters work best, but pennies will do in a pinch. (Is that a pun?)

The secret is using very strong glue, like epoxy glue, so have a grown-up help you. Make sure the glue has time to dry completely, too, or you will be loosing money every time you dance!

Just glue two or three coins on the soles and heels of each shoe. As soon as the glue dries, you're ready for action!

P.S. Thrift shops and dance schools sometimes sell outgrown tap shoes, so you might be able to pick up an inexpensive pair there, too.

GLUE COINS (PENNIES WILL DO) ON BOTTOM TOES AND HEELS OF OLD SHOES OR SNEAKERS

Tap dance language

Here are the basic movements of tap and soft shoe dancing (see page 54). But remember, reading about dancing is different from actually doing it. So get up on your feet, and give it a try!

Step: You do this one every day! It's just stepping down on one foot, like you do when you walk. Pick your foot up, and put it down — that's all there is to it.

Stamp: Even if you've never tap danced, you've surely stamped. To stamp, pick up a foot and stamp it hard in front of you.

Shuffle: Now that you're practically an expert, try a shuffle. Lift your foot off the floor a little, and kick it forward, slapping the sole of your foot on the floor as you do. Then pull it back, slapping your sole on the way back, too. The shuffle takes place on a quick count of 1-2.

When you practice shuffling, do it on one foot after the other, shifting your weight from one side to the other, and staying in place.

Slap: The slap couldn't be more simple. You give a tiny kick and slap your sole (and weight) down on the floor in front of you. Practice slapping, one foot after the other, and you'll find yourself moving forward. Slap across the room to practice this step.

Ball: Put the ball of your foot on the floor. Yup. That's the whole movement.

Heel: Lift your heel, without lifting the rest of your foot, and click it down on the floor. (We told you tap was easy!)

• THE TIME STEP •

Okay, hoofers, you're now ready to learn the *Time Step*, the tap dance step that's known to tap dancers all over the world. You can do the time step to any music with a 1-2-3-4 or 1-2 beat. Start ultra slow, and build up speed as you practice.

Stamp your right foot in front of you (putting your weight on it).

Pull back your right foot and click your left heel at the same time.

Step right (with weight on right).

Slap with left foot (change weight to left).

Step on right (with weight on right).

Now the pattern repeats on the left side:

Stamp on left (weight on left).

Pull back left foot as you click right heel.

Step left (weight on left).

Slap right (weight on right).

Step on left (with weight on left).

Then, stamp right, and so on, repeating pattern. (When you get used to the pattern, add some extra bounce to the stamp and pull back so the step will have its well-known pizzazz.)

To count out the time step, here are the steps connected to a 1-2-3-4 beat. The "Ands" and "A" get quick beats, too.

And	a	1	2	and 3	4
Stamp	Pull back	Click heel	Step	Slap	Stamp

• THE SOFT SHOE •

Soft Shoe dancing is a lot like tap dancing — without taps and at a slower pace. A perfect song for the soft shoe is *Tea for Two*. Ask a grown-up to teach you the melody or look for it in the library. "Shuffle, ball, step, step" is the easy pattern of this dance.

Start with a shuffle of your right foot;

then step on the ball of your right foot;

then step on your left foot, shifting the weight of your body to the left.

Then, step right again, shifting your weight right.

Your left foot is now free and ready for another shuffle, as the movements start again on the other side. It helps to count out the steps aloud, saying, "Shuffle, ball, step, step — shuffle, ball, step, step." Or, try it this way, "1-2-and 3-4, 1-2-and-3-4," over and over. Go slow at first, until you get the basic step down; then build up your speed.

Make a top hat

Dancing in a top hat and carrying a cane makes tap and soft shoe even more fun. To make a top hat, cut a strip of black poster board about 10" by 15" (depending on the size of your head). Staple it closed with the top end just a teensy bit smaller than the bottom.

Next, use a dinner plate to trace a large circle. Cut out the inside of the circle leaving a "brim" of about 3". The brim slides over the narrow part of the cylinder, but should fit tightly, about an inch before it gets to the end.

Voila! A top hat! If you have a pair of white gloves, wear them when you dance, too. An old cane or sturdy, straight stick painted black adds to the dance, too. You can "take a break" from the basic step you're doing to walk around the cane.

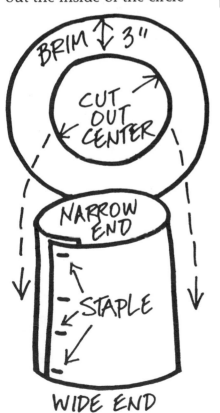

Get inspired

We're lucky to live in a time when great dancing has been captured on film. Some great dancers who used tap and soft shoe to express themselves are: Fred Astaire, Ginger Rogers, Gene Kelly, Shirley Temple, and Gregory Hines.

If you and your family rent movies, try watching some of these classics. They have tap dancing that is sure to inspire you! *Top Hat, The Good Ship Lollipop, That's Entertainment* (watch for the *Singing in the Rain* routine), and *Follow the Fleet*.

• HIP HOP •

How can we describe *hip hop*? That's the question that we asked of some hip hop fans around our town. Here's what they told us: "Hip hop is the beat. It's the hippest music coming down. It's a dance with a rappin' sound. It's a cool club beat. It's disco, rock, and rap together. *Hip hop* is magic on its feet. Give it a chance."

Hip hop evolved from break dancing, but took it one step further. It combined it with regular dancing to make something entirely new and different!

Try the dance

Hop up on your feet, and give a kick that's neat.

Then hand on the ground, and walk yourself around.

Jump up again and spin like a pin.

Listen to the sound, turn yourself around.

Let your elbows pop, never, ever stop.

You got it now. Hip hop!

• TAKE A MOON WALK •

1. RIGHT LEG BENDS LEFT LEG SLIDES BACK

2. TOES ARE POINTED WEIGHT SHIFTS FROM ONE LEG TO THE OTHER

3. OTHER LEG SLIDES AGAIN

The *Moon Walk* is a special dance that goes with rap music, too. It got its name because moon walking seems to defy gravity! A moon walker looks more like he's gliding across the moon than stepping here on earth.

To moon walk, bend your right knee and lift your right foot from the arch, sliding the foot backward. The left foot gets raised as the right one seems to "land" in back of you. Actually, you adjust its position so that it's just under you. The second your right heel hits the ground, begin lifting the left foot, and vice versa. In the moon walk, both legs are always in a state of changing position.

The secret of moon walking is super smooth movement as you work both legs simultaneously. Hold your arms as if they were floating out from you. Bob your head as if it were floating, too. You don't travel very far in this dance, even though it looks like you are walking. That's part of the optical illusion of the moon walk!

• FLAMENCO! •

Flamenco dancing comes from southern Spain. It's dancing that's done with loud, clicking heels and toes, and lots of dramatic flair! Every move in flamenco is definite and strong. When you put your toe down, jab it down. When you click your heel, click it with strength. Flamenco is a dance of passion and high energy!

The look of flamenco

Ladies sometimes dance with a rose in their teeth or stuck behind one ear. They wear bright-colored dresses that hug their bodies and flair out at the knees. Their hair is usually tied back in a knot.

Men dress like matadors!

Flamenco steps

Step on toe, click heel down, step on toe, click heel down, step on toe, click heel down! Continue, building speed until your clicking heels sound faster than a woodpecker's tapping.

Throw your arms up over your head, pressing your palms firmly against each other and click your heels like crazy! Let out a shout of *Viva!* or *Arriba!* ("live!" and "up!" in Spanish). Living and feeling "up" is what flamenco is all about!

Make walnut castanets

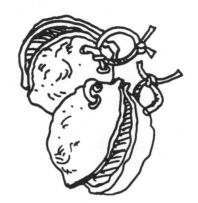

Castanets are small, hand-held instruments that add to the clicking of flamenco. One of the ways to make them is with walnut shells.

Open a walnut and empty out the meat inside (delicious!). Use a small nail to tap a hole in the upper end of each shell. With strong thread (coat quality, or nylon), tie the shells together.

Wooden spoon castanets

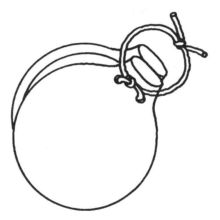

If you have two identical wooden spoons to spare, you can make castanets from them, too. Ask a grown-up to saw off the handles almost to the end, near the bulb. Make two small holes in what's left of the handles and attach a short piece of fishing tackle or strong thread.

Snap and clack!

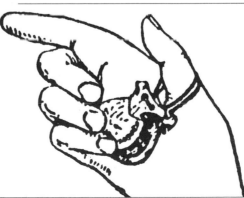

To play the castanets, hold a set in each hand, and bending your palm together, make them click. The secret is keeping your fingers together and your hand half closed at all times. Fantastico!

MUSICAL TOYS

• MAGICAL MUSIC FROM DRINKING GLASSES •

Drinking glasses, especially ones made with real crystal, create some of the loveliest sounds around. All you need to create these sparkling sounds are glasses, water, and metal spoons. (It helps to keep a sponge on hand, too, to pick up little spills.)

Ask for permission to use the very best glasses you can find for this project. Thin, delicate glass makes a more musical sound than thick glass.

(No drinking glasses? Try glass bottles to create this music.)

• TWO SPARKLING SONGS •

To play these songs, you'll need three glasses, each filled with three different levels of water to make different sounds.

The more water you put in the glass, the lower the sound it will make. Experiment with water levels until you find the first three notes of *Mary Had a Little Lamb*, or *Hot Cross Buns*. Once you have them, put them in order of high, middle, low. You can call those sounds 3 (high), 2 (middle), and 1(low).

When you tap, remember, less is definitely more. The more gentle the touch, the more sparkling the sound. Relax your hand and let the spoon swing freely.

Mary Had a Little Lamb

Mary Had a Little Lamb, or *Merrily We Roll Along* is perfect for your first drinking glass concert. With just three notes, the musical code is very easy to follow. When a number is written in dark type, hold that note longer than the rest.

3 2 1 2 3 3 **3**
Ma-ry had a lit-tle lamb

2 2 **2**   3 3 **3**
Lit-tle lamb, lit-tle lamb

3 2 1 2 3 3 3
Ma-ry had a lit-tle lamb

3 2   2 3 2 **1**
Its fleece was white as snow

Hot Cross Buns

You can play *Hot Cross Buns* on the same three glasses as *Mary Had a Little Lamb*.

3   2   **1**
Hot cross   buns

3   2   **1**
Hot cross   buns

1   1   1 1
One   a   pen-ny

2   2   2   2
Two   a   pen-ny

3   2   **1**
Hot   cross   buns

Once you're an experienced drinking glass player, it's time to try something really fantastic — creating your own crystal concert!

AN ENCHANTING CRYSTAL CONCERT

Making crystal concerts is fun anytime, but for birthdays and special occasions, they're the best! There's no greater gift than music.

For the concert, you'll need to make eight notes that go down in a row, which is called a *scale*. An easy way to find the right notes is to think of the first line of the Christmas carol, "Joy to the world, the Lord is come." Those notes go down the scale, one by one. Test by tapping the glasses, and adjusting the amount of water in them, until you find the right notes.

If you are making your concert as a surprise, set up the things you need in advance in a safe place, so they'll be ready to play when you announce the concert. If you set up the concert a day in advance, use a marker to show how much liquid to put in each glass.

Play on a rainbow!

To make your concert even more heavenly, put a few drops of food coloring in each glass for a shimmering rainbow effect. Your eight notes will make a beautiful rainbow when you put these colors in this order (for math lovers, we've given them numbers, too):

clear	red	orange	yellow	green	blue	purple	clear
1	2	3	4	5	6	7	8

Remember:　red plus yellow makes orange
blue plus yellow makes green
red plus blue makes purple

Under each glass, put a paper with the number of the tone that glass plays.

Twinkle, Twinkle, Little Star, played on a rainbow

clear	green	blue	green
1,1	5,5	6,6	**5**

Twin-kle,　twin-kle,　lit-tle　staaaaar

yellow	orange	red	clear
4,4	3,3	2,2	**1**

How I　won-der　what you　aaaaare

green	yellow	orange	red
5,5	4,4	3,3	**2**

Up a-　bove the　world so　high

green	yellow	orange	red
5,5	4,4	3,3	**2**

Like a　dia-mond　in the　skyyyyyy

clear	green	blue	green
1,1	5,5	6,6	**5**

Twin-kle,　twin-kle,　lit-tle　staaaaar

yellow	orange	red	clear
4,4	3,3	2,2	**1**

How I　won-der　what you　aaaaare

Amazing Grace

Miracles are for real — that's what this song is about. Your listeners will believe it, too, when they hear this sparkling song. We've put in a harmony to add, when you're ready. Tap two notes at the same time to make harmony. Remember that numbers written in bold are held longer.

clear	blue	{blue,green,yellow}	blue	green	yellow
1	**4**	{6-5-4}	**6**	5	**4**
A -	ma-	zing	grace	how	sweet

red	clear	clear	yellow	{blue,green,yellow)
2	**1**	1	**4**	{6-5-4}
the	sound,	That	saved	a

blue,	green	clear (top)
6	5	**8**
wretch	like	me!

clear top,	clear	blue	blue	green
8	**8** (har. 6)	**6**	6 (harmony 4)	5
I	once	was	lost	but

yellow	red	clear	clear	yellow
4	2	**1**	1	**4**
now	I'm	found.	Was	blind

blue	blue	green	yellow
6	**6** (harmony 4)	5 (harmony 3)	**4**
but	now	I	see!

The Disney classic, *I'm Wishing*, from the movie *Snow White*, is fantastic on glasses, too, if you drop number 7 (blue) down a little. You do this by spilling just a little bit of water out. Tapping the glasses with a rubber mallet creates a lovely echo.

A CRAZY COLLECTION OF HOMEMADE CLASSICS

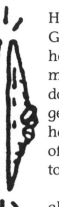

Horns! Drums! Maracas! Guitars! They're in your house now, free for the making. All you have to do is find the fixings and get to work. Soon, you'll have a whole orchestra full of homemade instruments to play.

These instruments have all stood the test of time, too. Generations of kids have had fun crafting them, and playing them. Now it's your turn, music maker! Get ready to raid the recyclables, and create some classics of your own!

One, two, doodle-dee doo! Honk! Honk! Boom! Make music!

Once you've created some of the instruments on the next few pages, you'll be ready to rock and roll, twist and shout, jump and jive!

You can shake 'em, pound 'em, beat 'em, tap 'em, blow 'em. Shake 'em hard, shake 'em soft, bang 'em high, bang 'em low! Use your hands, use your feet, have a parade, and keep the beat!

Macaroni-box fiddle with a butter-knife bow

Remove the see-through window from an elbow macaroni box, and paint the box a bright color. When it's dry, string rubber bands over it, the long way.

Next, take a flattened, painted spaghetti box (with ends removed), and fold it lengthwise. Attach it to the bottom of the elbow macaroni box with staples, or tape.

Make a *bridge*, by cutting a slit in the box, to hold the bands up. From an end flap of the spaghetti box, cut a T-shape and insert it in the slit. The bridge keeps the strings from hitting the box, so it can make a richer sound.

To play, put the box under your chin, being careful not to touch the rubber bands. Hold the rubber bands up with your thumb and forefinger. Pluck with your fingers, or fiddle with a butter-knife bow.

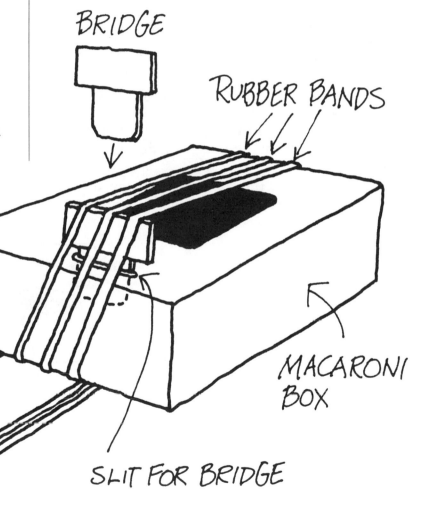

BRIDGE

RUBBER BANDS

SPAGHETTI BOX

MACARONI BOX

SLIT FOR BRIDGE

Tissue box lute and shoe box guitar

These instruments are simple to create and play, but more importantly, they make a really great sound. The secret is using different sizes of rubber bands, thick and thin, for the strings.

Shoe box guitar: String the rubber bands across the long end of the box. Thick rubber bands make low tones when plucked. Thin ones make higher tones. Three or four bands on one box are about the right number.

We know a kid who created a box that happened to play the exact three notes needed for *Hot Cross Buns*! Try out the tones on your guitar. Is there a song you can play on it?

Tissue box lute: Tissue boxes make some of the best lutes and harps around because they have a ready-made hole in the middle that's just right for the sound to roll around in before it comes out.

Stretch rubber bands around the box, the short way, and pluck. You have just created a simple, but lovely instrument.

RUBBER BANDS

TISSUE BOX LUTE

Shakers, maracas, and tube horns

Coffee can shakers: All you need for this is an empty metal can with a lid and a handful of dried rice or beans. Put the beans in the can, cover tightly, and shake, shake, shake!

Paper bag maracas: These maracas look and sound like the real thing. Start by decorating paper bags — the brighter the colors you use, the better. Fill them with dried beans and tie with yarn. Now, shake, shake, shake! These colorful time keepers are terrific in a *Brazilian Carnival* (see *Multicultural Party*, page 146).

Cardboard tubing horns: Paint paper tubes and decorate them. Then, sing into them for an easy to make — and play — home-made horn. You can even make a royal bugle by taping the edge of a colorful scarf onto the side of a long gift wrap tube, and sounding a royal fanfare.

Dancing bells

This is an instrument you can wear, that's perfect for shaking or dancing, especially circle dancing. To make it, sew two or three jingle bells onto a strip of elastic — the kind you can buy in any fabric shop or dime store — or tie them onto a piece of strong string. (Color the elastic with water color paint if you want.) Then sew the elastic ends together (or tie them, or the string) to make a band that can slip onto your arm or ankle.

Make a few dancing bells at a time. Different-sized bells make different sounds, too.

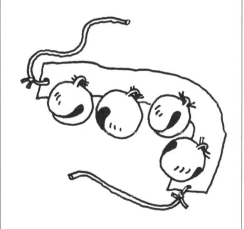

• TWO COOL BASS FIDDLES •

You can make your own bass (pro-nounced "base") fiddles to keep time to music. These instruments work in all kinds of music from jazz (see *What's Your Style*, page 104) to jug band (see *Sharing the Fun*, page 134).

Basic Bass Fiddle: The first thing you have to do to create this bass is to eat a lot of oatmeal or grits! That's because the large round boxes these foods come in make the best sounds. (If you can't find a round box, a rectangular one will do in a pinch.)
What you'll need:

a large box

a small piece of thick cardboard

a piece of string, or a thin shoelace

First, cut out a circular piece of thick cardboard, about three inches across, to serve as a kind of "washer." Pierce the cardboard and the bottom of the cereal box in the center, with a nail.

Tie a knot on one end of the shoelace — a thin round one is best. Thread the lace first through the "washer," and next up through the bottom of the box. Presto! You've got a bass.

To play the bass, hold the bottom firmly with your foot, or if you have a volunteer, ask him to hold it down while you play. Wrap the free end of the string around your hand. Pluck the bass string with your free hand. You can vary the sound by holding the string in different places, and holding it looser or tighter. The tighter it is, the higher the sound.

Bungee bass: This one could fool a professional musician — that's how good it sounds. To make it, you need one cardboard carton, open at the top, and an elastic cable or bungee. Hook the bungee on opposite sides of the carton. To play, hold the bungee up and pluck.

CUT CARDBOARD (THE THICKER THE BETTER)

← STRING

← KNOT END

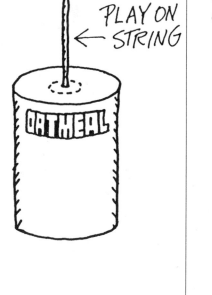

MAKE HOLE WITH NAIL

OATMEAL

PULL STRING UP

KNOT END

PLAY ON → STRING

OATMEAL

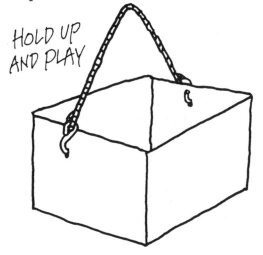

HOLD UP AND PLAY

2 x 4 guitar

Any board about two feet long will do. Space three or four nails a few inches from the top and the bottom of the board. Line the nails up with each other and with the nails on the other end of the board.

To make a bridge, nail and glue in a rectangular piece of wood, about $1\frac{1}{2}$ inches by 4 inches, across the board. (Put glue on the bottom of the bridge, and nail from the back.)

String with rubber bands for a great hand-held guitar!

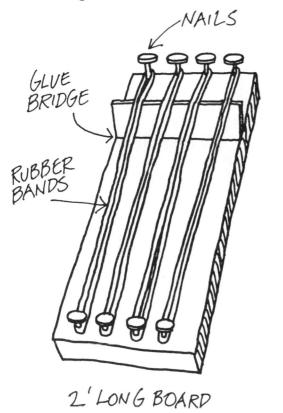

NAILS

GLUE BRIDGE

RUBBER BANDS

2' LONG BOARD

6" RULER

COFFEE CAN

RUBBER BANDS

Coffee can harp

A bunch of rubber bands and some empty coffee cans also make good instruments. Just wrap bands of different sizes around each can, making sure that the bands don't touch each other. Insert a six-inch ruler as a bridge, if you want. Then pluck the can harp to find the best sounds in it. The different thicknesses of the rubber bands will create different pitches. Turn the can over and pluck the bands on the bottom, too. They ping!

Clay pot bells

Tie a knot around a small stick at one end of a piece of thin rope; then string the free end through the inside of a clay flowerpot. Hold the string up so that the pot is free, and strike it gently with a wooden spoon. Pots of different sizes make different tones. Thin ones make clearer tones than thick ones.

If you have more than two pots, use a strong wooden hanger to tie them on. Play by holding the hanger high and tapping lightly with a mallet.

PULL STRING UP

• SOMETHING SPECIAL •

Metal tube xylophones

This instrument takes more time and effort to make than some of the other instruments, but the rich sound it makes is worth it! You'll need a grown-up, a hacksaw, a metal drill bit, a 6'–8' piece of metal tubing, some strong string or fishing tackle, and a sturdy dowel (stick) 2'–3' long, to hang the tubes on.

If you don't have a handy grown-up available at home or some of the tools, you might find them at your local hardware store or plumbing supply store (where they sell metal tubing). Someone there may be willing to cut the metal into pipes and drill two small holes near the top of each tube for you. Make your longest tube a foot long, with the others each slightly smaller, in progression. The shortest one can be about 8". A 6'–8' tube can make 6–9 different pipes or notes for your xylophone.

Run the string through the holes of each tube and tie it onto the straight stick. Strike with a rubber mallet.

Ahhh, what music!

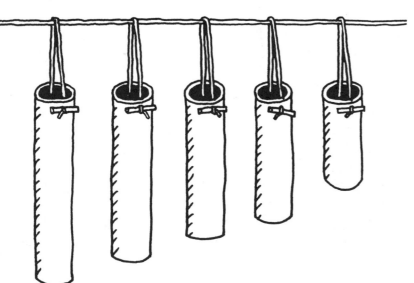

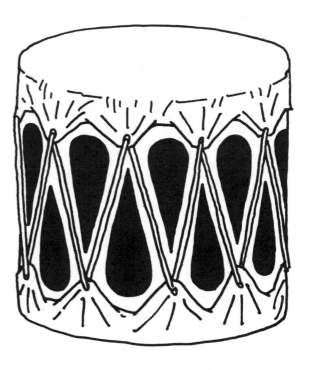

A CHAMOIS DRUM: YOUR LASTING TREASURE

A drum made from chamois (SHAM-mee) is one homemade instrument that is made to last. Like the metal pipes, making this drum will take more effort than some of the other instruments in this section. But your reward for the work will be a very special instrument that can serve you for a long time with good care.

Chamois is sheep skin finished with cod oil. Because it comes from an animal, chamois — and the drum it will become — need to be treated with respect.

Use a large metal drum, like a two-pound coffee can, open at both ends. The larger the can, the bolder the drum. (Pizza places often have cans this size.)

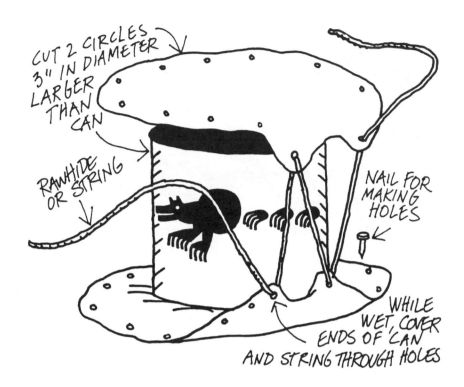

CUT 2 CIRCLES 3" IN DIAMETER LARGER THAN CAN

RAWHIDE OR STRING

NAIL FOR MAKING HOLES

WHILE WET, COVER ENDS OF CAN AND STRING THROUGH HOLES

Paint the can and decorate it with colors and symbols that have special meaning for you.

Cut two circles of chamois at least three inches in diameter larger than the top of the can. Working on an old board, make evenly spaced holes around the circles with a fat nail.

Once the holes are made, soak the chamois in icy cold water until it becomes rubbery to the touch (about 20 minutes). *While it is still wet,* cover the ends of the drum, and string rawhide, gimp, or strong string through the holes, pulling as tightly as you can. Tie the rawhide or string tightly and wait for the chamois to dry (24 hours). As it dries, it will shrink, making the drumhead even tighter.

The drum you create will last a very long time, and have special meaning, because it was created with care — by you.

Beat Boppers — carton drums that can be beat!

These are simple drums to make, but guess what? Beat boppers sound great! Turn over an empty carton and strike it with a large wooden spoon or a homemade mallet. Or, use the carton as a drum machine, drumming on the insides of the box to keep a basic beat. To make a parade drum, see page 125.

• MAKING MALLETS •

The all-time best drumstick is a simple rubber spatula — the kind cooks use to scrape out a bowl — but a wooden spoon works well, too. If you'd like to make a better looking mallet, here are some suggestions.

For the stick, use chopsticks, or dowels, or hardwood tree (maple, ash, oak) sticks, as straight as you can find. Paint or varnish them, if you like.

For the knobs, wind strips of felt soaked in white glue around the tip of each stick. Or, try a nylon stocking or plastic bag pulled tight and twisted around the top of the stick. Tuck and tie the end, or attach with string.

Swish mallets

This kind of mallet makes great special effects on kettle or snare drums. The simplest is a basting brush from the kitchen. Or, make a swish mallet with a bunch of broom straws tied together or an old whisk broom, cut in half.

PIECE OF DOWEL STICK →

BROOM STRAWS

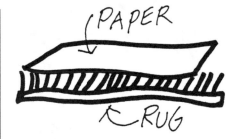

PAPER

RUG

The world's simplest snare drum

A snare drum has a special razzmatazz sound that comes from stings or "snares" on its bottom. You can create something very close to that sound by making the World's Simplest Snare Drum. All you need is a room with a thick carpet, one piece of loose-leaf paper, and a pencil or two. Put the paper on the carpet and drum with the pencil.

A snare drum beat

Try creating this rhythm with two pencils on your homemade snare:
Ricka Ticka Ticka
Ricka Ticka Ticka
Ricka Ticka Ticka
Tim Buk Tu

An instant kettle drum

Strike a metal cookie sheet with a rubber mallet for a bodacious kettle drum!

Pie plate tambourines

A few jiggling keys, paper clips, buttons, and bells can transform a pie pan right out of the recyclables and into a show! Just punch holes on the side of the plate with a hole puncher. Use metal wire twists to attach any small objects that will jiggle when the tambourine is shaken. Long thin ribbons or thick yarn strung through a few holes adds to the effect.

Make two, and you'll have *cymbals* to crash!

Terrific teaspoon timekeepers

Just a teaspoon in each hand will give you a terrific timekeeper when you're making music. Tap the rounded parts of the spoons together as you sing!

Bamboo flute

This is a homemade instrument with a lot of class and a great sound. All it takes is a tube of bamboo wood about a foot long, and a drill with a $^3/_{16}$" bit. Ask a grown-up to drill a hole about $1^1/_2$" from the end of the tube; this is where you will blow.

For an instrument that's unique to you, mark the places where your fingers fit comfortably on the tube and drill the finger holes there. File any rough spots with an emery board.

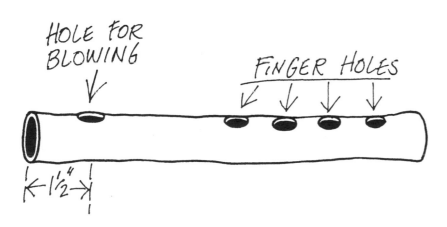

HOLE FOR BLOWING
↓

FINGER HOLES
↓ ↓ ↓ ↓

←1½"→

• GO COCONUTS! •

You can make a few different instruments from coconuts — and have something good to eat at the same time! Make sure that you buy coconuts that aren't cracked. Then, ask a grown-up to saw them in half for you, across the middle. Drink the milk and eat the white part. Then you'll have a coconut shell all ready to become a drum or clacker!

A coconut drum

To make a coconut drum, make sure the edges of your coconut half are fairly smooth. You can sand them with sandpaper. Then, get the largest balloon you can find, cut off the part you blow into and through it away, and stretch the remaining piece over the rim of the shell. Presto! A coconut bongo drum! (Please be sure to throw any bits and pieces of balloons away, as they are very dangerous to young children. Thank you.)

Coconut clappers

Coconut halves make great clappers, too. Just bump the rounded ends together for a rich "bonk" sound. This works best when you remove the "hair" from the shell.

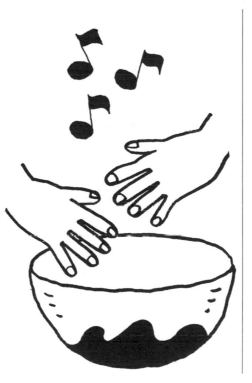

• DECORATE YOUR INSTRUMENTS •

The musical instruments you make are even more fun to use when they're decorated to look beautiful or funny or silly or unusual. Start by using poster paint, glitter, and stencils on the boxes you've chosen to make music with. A dash of dish-washing soap (just an eensy bit) in poster paint will make painting over glossy boxes easier. While you paint, color, and draw on your soon-to-be instruments, be sure to have music playing to inspire you. Let your creativity take control! Use colors so bright and designs so wild that the instruments will seem to play themselves! They'll probably look so good you'll want a photo of them!

A musical safari — right in your own home!

Calling all adventurers! How many *other* potential musical instruments are lurking around your house? Go on a hunt and we bet you'll discover something new!

Your mission is to go from room to room looking for anything that might make an interesting sound. Collect any bells, whistles, pot lids, and pans that make a good sound when banged with a wooden spoon. Try to find Dad's old harmonica and the kazoo you once got as a party favor.

Here are some often-overlooked objects with good musical potential:

Snorkeling gear: The rubber tubes make interesting saxophones when you blow or sing into the hard end.

Baby toys: These often have music boxes and bells in them.

Funnels: They have great potential as amplifiers for any horn-type instruments you make.

And don't forget *bicycle horns, jingle bells, an old-fashioned washboard, combs, hairbrushes,* and even *clumps of keys!*

Once you've discovered all the musical stuff in the house, have fun experimenting, making all the sounds you can!

HOMEMADE JAM

Once you have your collection of crazy homemade instruments, it's time to *jam*! No, we don't mean the stuff you put on bread! *Jam* is the word musicians use when they are getting together to make music. Homemade instruments are perfect for *jamming* when friends come over. Just put on some music and play along with it!

And after that, you can have a parade, using all the instruments you made! Or, you can put on a jug band show (see page 135).

P.S. Don't worry if your friends are a little rough on your homemade instruments. They only have to last as long as the *jam session* does. And besides, half the fun of making them is making more. The other half is — you guessed it — playing them!

Music makes me hungry!

When you invite your friends to jam with you, ask them to bring along a jar of their favorite jam or jelly to eat! Music makers get hungry, and it's fun to see which flavors other people like best.

• SIMPLE SIMON'S INSTRUMENTS •

Here's a fun game to play with friends, after you've made a bunch of instruments. One of you gets to be Simon, the leader of the band. The others are band members who do what Simon does.

Simon gets three instruments to make rhythm on — but the band is only supposed to follow two of them. The other is special — for Simon's solos. If Simon plays "rat-a-tat-tat" on instrument one or two, the band members respond "rat-a-tat-tat." But, if Simon plays a rhythm on instrument three, the band members respond with silence! If band members follow Simon when she plays the third instrument, they're out!

P.S. We'd love to know what else you discover when you make homemade instruments. Creativity is what music is all about, and we'll bet you come up with lots of good ideas of your own. Drop us a line (Music makers, c/o Williamson Publishing, P.O. Box 185, Charlotte, VT 05445) and tell us about them!

No jam today?

If there's no one around to make music with, put on a CD, record, tape, or the radio. There you'll find the greatest musicians in the world, ready to jam with you! Just pick up your instrument and play — and sing — along with the greats!

• BE A ONE-KID BAND •

When you've made some homemade instruments, it's time to strike up the band! But what if you're playing by yourself that day? That's the perfect time to be a *one-kid band*.

Being a one-kid band means playing as many instruments as you can manage at one time. In fact, the more, the better!

How about having a carton to kick as a drum, while your hands take turns honking a bike horn and ringing a bell? (You may want to sit in a chair if you use a carton drum. That way you can hit it on the top with your heel without kicking it away from you.)

If you have a chair with slats in the house, use it to tie instruments on, and for striking with a wooden spoon or rubber mallet. A drum under your elbow will make use of another part of you, too. Once you've got your instruments lined up where you can reach them, you're ready to go!

The one-kid band presents The Blue Danube

The Blue Danube, a song about a beautiful river in Eastern Europe, is perfect for a one-kid band. It has a strong 1-2-3 (waltz) beat, a well-known, easy melody with plenty of room for honks and toots. Perform *The Blue Danube* by singing "la, la, la" or by whistling. If you don't know the tune, ask a grown-up.

The Blue Danube

We put plunk plunks, honk honks, booms, and a ding in this version, but of course, as a one-kid band you'll choose your own sounds.

La, la, la, la, laaaaaaa (plunk, plunk) (honk honk)

La, la, la, la, laaaaaaa (plunk, plunk) (honk honk)

La, la, la, la, laaaaaaaaaa (boom boom) (honk honk)

La, la, la, la, laaaaaaa (boom boom) (honk honk)

La, la, la, la, laaaaaa! (plunk plunk) (boom boom)

La, la, la, la, laaaaaaa! (boom boom) (honk honk)

La, la, la, la, la

La, la, (ring bell) *laaaaaaaaa!*

La, la, la, (quick boom) *la, la,* (quick boom) *la, la* (ding ding ding!)

Bicycle Built for Two

Here's another one-kid band favorite, with a tune someone in your home or school is sure to know. This one is good for singing, too.

Daisy, Daisy

Give me your answer do (honk, honk)

I'm half crazy

All for the love of you (ding ding)

It won't be a stylish marriage (boom)

I can't afford a carriage (boom boom)

But you'd look sweet (ding)

Upon the seat (ding)

Of a bicycle built for two! (honk honk!)

• AN ACCIDENTAL ORCHESTRA •

After you've created a bunch of instruments why not organize them into sections, like a real orchestra? Think in terms of *stringed* instruments, which you pluck to make sound. Or *wind* instruments, which you blow into for sound. *Percussion* instruments make rhythms when you beat them or shake them. Here's an example of how you might organize your orchestra of homemade instruments.

In the stringed section:
  Macaroni box fiddle
  Oatmeal box bass fiddle
  Tissue box guitar
  Shoe box guitar
  Bungee carton bass

In the wind section:
  Snorkeling gear sax
  Paper towel tube horn

In the percussion section:
  Paper bag and coffee can maracas
  Beat bopper drum
  Coconut drums and clappers
  Teaspoon timekeepers
  Pie plate tambourines and cymbals

Be the conductor

To conduct, or lead, your accidental orchestra, turn to pages 107 and 108. It's great fun!

Let the music play

You can conduct old favorites with your accidental orchestra — familiar songs, like *I've Been Working on the Railroad, Skip to My Lou,* and *Old MacDonald Had a Farm.*

But it's also fun to play along with some of your favorite taped music. As the conductor, your job is to keep time by waving your hand with the beat of the music.

Discovering new music to play along with may be the most fun of all. How about turning on the radio to a kind of music you like but have never heard before? See how your accidental orchestra does playing along with that!

The parade's in town!

Your accidental orchestra can be a parade, too! Just get up on your feet and start sounding off (see *Make a Parade,* page 125).

• MAKE A BOOM-BAH •

What's that? You never heard of a *boom-bah*? Well, then you've never visited the Leather Corner Post Hotel and Restaurant in Fogelsville, Pennsylvania. That's the "Home of the Boom-bahs," where people boom and bah every Friday night. But don't worry. You don't have to go to Pennsylvania to find a boom-bah. You can make one of your very own! That's what folks in Fogelsville do, and they should know — they invented boom-bahs!

Boom-bahs are like people — each and every one is a unique creation, never to be duplicated. An old pogo stick is the ideal spine for this unique instrument, but a broom stick with an auto spring and rubber foot (the kind you find on stool legs) on the end does fine, too. (If you don't have a rubber foot, play the boom-bah inside a carton or glue felt to the bottom, and it won't make marks on the floor.) Once you've got the spine

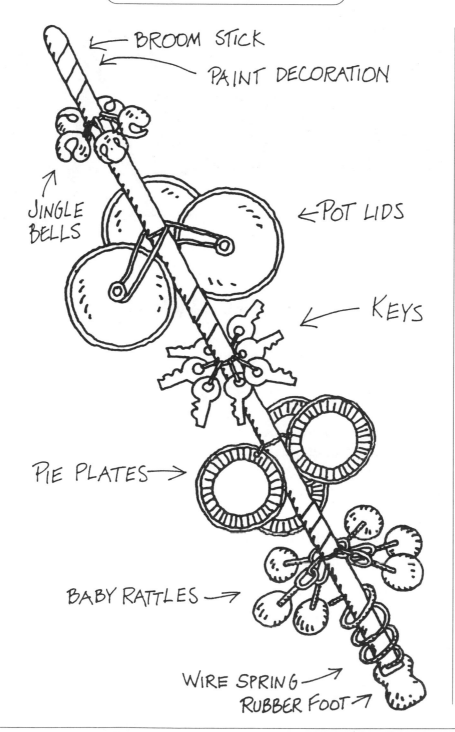

BROOM STICK

PAINT DECORATION

JINGLE BELLS

←POT LIDS

← KEYS

PIE PLATES →

BABY RATTLES →

WIRE SPRING →

RUBBER FOOT →

painted and gussied up, and ready for booming, it's time to add on the bahs — jingling keys, bells, bottle caps — any noise maker you can think of. Attach them with the strong, round staples used to hold telephone wires, or nail things loosely on the stick.

Playing the boom-bah

Playing the boom-bah isn't very hard — but it is a lot of fun! All you do is thump it on the floor, while singing your heart out to the beat. The more boom-bahs, the better, too. So why not invite some friends over for a boom-bah-making party, followed by lots of booming and bahhing.

At the Leather Corner Post Hotel and Restaurant, boom-bahhers stomp along to songs on the juke box, to every style of song, from polka to disco. You and your boom-bah group can do the same, to tapes or the radio. Most of all have fun, which is the secret to successful boom-bahhing and successful music making, too, for that matter!

Nature's Music

MUSIC IS EVERYWHERE

When you walk in the woods on a sunny, spring day, or sit by a pond on a hot, summer night, you can hear one of the greatest orchestras around — for free! When it comes to making music, Mother Nature is right up there with the best! Birds chirp and whistle in the treetops. Frogs bellow to their loves — nature has a thousand sounds!

How many different kinds of nature's music can you think of? Can you think of three? Five? Ten? Here's one to get you started — waves lapping at the shore. Now, it's your turn!

Season sounds

Each season has its own special music.

In spring, birds twitter.

In summer, insects hum.

In fall, leaves dance to the ground.

Winter winds howl.

What season is it now? What special sounds come with that season?

MUSICAL SEASON STORIES

You can make a musical story for whatever season is around you. Here's how:

Put on some music that has no words, and act out the events of a season. Let your imagination run free!

For a spring story, you can pretend to be a flower sprouting up from the earth. Start as a seed curled up in the ground and use the music to straighten up and bloom! If you have a friend to play with, she can be a butterfly or bird who flits around the flower.

For the summer story, you can be a chirping cricket, a frog in a bog, or even the hot sun crossing the sky. How about a thunderstorm?

In the fall story, leaves twist and fall in the wind. Pretend you are a leaf, drifting in the wind to the ground.

For winter, be a snowflake tumbling down from the sky, or the cold wind blowing, or a dancing snowman who starts to melt when the sun comes out!

Timeless inspiration

The classical composer Vivaldi was inspired by the changing seasons, too. He created *The Four Seasons*, a wonderful piece of classical music that you can find in the library. Use it as background music for your season stories. Or listen to it with your family and talk about how the music makes you feel.

Translate the sounds of nature

There are lots of ways to express the music you hear in nature. How about grabbing some colored pencils and paper and drawing what you hear? Musical sounds and feelings can become wonderful works of art — by you!

Don't feel like drawing? Why not write about the way you feel when you hear the sounds of nature? If you write a poem, you might even find it turns into a *lyric* later on!

LIGHTS! ACTION! LIFE!

Being alive and part of this world is one giant, supreme, and wonderful miracle. From the moment we're born we're feeling, exploring, and finding our way. What an experience! What an adventure! And what a big job!

Sometimes, being human can seem overwhelming. One day, you're full of joy, the sky is blue, and life is rosy. Another day there are storm clouds overhead, you have a fight with your best friend, and life feels kind of gloomy.

Fortunately, nature — our own human nature, that is — gave us a few ways to deal with the roller coaster feelings that come with being alive. One way is having special people in our lives — that's called love.

Another important way is called art. Art is how we express the way we feel. Art is how we show others what's going on deep inside of us, and how we come to understand what it is we are feeling.

Art can be painting, drawing, sculpture, creative writing, theater, music, or dance. It's any creative activity done to express what's happening inside a person's heart and soul.

Because music can express so much about what it is to be human, it's a great art — maybe even the greatest.

It's kind of hard to imagine life without it, isn't it?

No wonder people the world over listen to and play music every day! But the luckiest people of all, of course, are the ones who actually get to make music — people like you!

A MUSICAL WEATHER REPORT

If weather were music, what would a sunny day sound like? Can you make up a sound for fluffy clouds, floating across the sky?

How about a stormy night with thunder and lightning? How would you make the sound of rain in music?

What is the weather like now, at this very moment? If today's weather were musical, what would it sound like? If you were writing a song about it, what would you say?

WRITING LYRICS

Lyrics are words set to music. Often, a song will be inspired by a few simple words filled with sincere feelings, or a *phrase* that comes into the songwriter's mind. The words set the mood and get your creative feelings going.

In music, think of saying more with fewer words. Every word in a lyric counts, and the fewer you need to express what you're feeling, the deeper your lyric is apt to strike people.

If you think up words before you come up with a tune, just make sure that the music you create has a beat for each *syllable* (every separate sound) of the words you're setting to music.

And if you think of a melody first, make sure your words match the number of notes in the tune.

For instance, the tune to *Row, Row, Row Your Boat* doesn't fit with the words, "Paddle, Paddle, Paddle, my brother's row boat," does it? But, put it with, "Yes, Yes, Yes, My Friend" and you've got something going!

Matching the number of notes to the number of syllables is the main rule of lyric writing. Lyrics will often rhyme, but they don't always have to.

• INSTRUMENTS FROM NATURE •

Our ancestors didn't have recorders or harmonicas, guitars or pianos to play on, but it didn't stop them from making music. They created music from the feelings inside them and whatever they could find in nature. They learned to make music the way we do today, by plucking, blowing, and striking.

A boy in the Stone Age may have found an animal bone with a hole in it and blown into it. The lovely sounds that came out would have delighted him. He might have experimented, adding more holes until he had a kind of flute to play. That's probably how wood-winds were first created.

A girl in the Stone Age may have come across the horn of a fallen ram and blown into it. Presto! The first horn!

An ancient hunter may have discovered that when he plucked his bow string, the result was musical. After a few centuries, that led to the creation of stringed instruments, like guitars and violins!

I HEAR BELLS

Ringing rocks

In eastern Pennsylvania, there's a park called Ringing Rocks. Visitors who go to this unusual park bring hammers with them, because if you strike a rock there, it makes a musical ringing sound! The secret is the high iron content of the rocks. If you know a place with a lot of rocks, try banging them with a hammer. You just may discover that there are ringing rocks where you live, too!

• MAKE A STONE AGE ORCHESTRA •

The stuff of nature is still around us, and it can still help bring out the music inside us. For fun, go outside and pretend that you live in the Stone Age. What musical instruments can you make and use that would express your musical feelings?

PULL OUT INNER PART →

SLICE AND NOTCH ↘

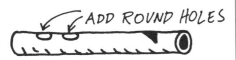

ADD ROUND HOLES

Make a willow whistle

The early settlers learned to make willow whistles from Native American children. Willow whistles are flutes that sound like the wind.

To make one, find a fat willow stick in springtime when the sap is running. Soak the stick in water for about an hour; then, gently twist and pull the inner part until it comes free of the bark.

Cut a diagonal slice from the top of the stick, and make a notch on the side. Add two round holes to make different tones. Go outside and whistle by the trees.

Pumpkin vine bassoon

In Fall, find the fattest pumpkin vine around and hollow it out with a nut pick. Make a thumbhole on the back of it, and two other holes in front. By covering the holes, you can make different notes.

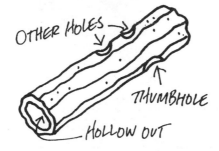

OTHER HOLES

THUMBHOLE

HOLLOW OUT

A tree branch harp

This instrument isn't strictly Stone Age, but it sure sounds good! Find a fallen branch in a Y-shape, and put rubber bands across the top of the Y. You'll have a wonderful, primitive harp!

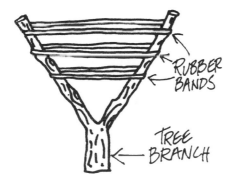

RUBBER BANDS

TREE BRANCH

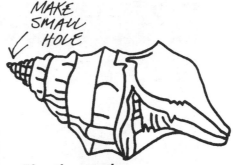

MAKE SMALL HOLE

Play the conch

Stone Age people discovered that shells can make good instruments. If you have a shell and can make a small hole in the end, give it a blow. If the shell belongs to somebody else, make sure you get permission first. To change the sound in a large shell, put your fist inside as you blow.

DRY FOR 4 MONTHS

Gourds make good shakers

At pumpkin time, buy a few gourds. Put them in a warm, dry place. Then wait — for about four months! The insides will dry out, leaving the seeds to shake around inside.

Grass or feather whistle

Some flat grasses can make whistling sounds if you stretch them across your mouth and blow. The most talented grasses for whistling are the wide, flat kind.

Watery sounds

Maurice Ravel, Antonio Vivaldi, and Claude Debussy were music makers who put the sounds of nature in their compositions. Listen to Debussy's *The Sea (La Mer)*, Vivaldi's *Storm at Sea*, and Ravel's *Water Games (Jeux d'Eau)*. You will hear how these great musicians made the sounds of water come alive through music.

• INSPIRED BY THE SKY! •

The sun, moon, clouds, and stars have inspired people to make music ever since time began. How many songs can you come up with that have the names of these heavenly bodies in them? Sing or hum the answers. Here are a few to get you started:

Moon River

Here Comes the Sun

When You Wish Upon a Star

There are plenty of other sky songs, especially if you look at the words of the songs, and not just the titles. See how many songs you and your friends and family can come up with. Keep a list going on your refrigerator and let others add to it, or make a poster to hang on your door.

Bird Song Creations

You can team up with one of Mother Nature's very best singers to create music. It's fun to do, and the results can be amazing! All you have to do is find a singing bird and listen to it. Then try to sing or whistle what you hear! Because you are a human, you won't sound exactly like the bird.

You may even want to learn to recognize bird calls. It's great fun to recognize the call of the plump Mourning Dove or the fiery red Cardinal, and it is good training for your "ear," because you'll have to listen carefully. Ask in your library for a recording of bird calls. Or, maybe a nearby wildlife preserve or Audubon Center will have a special birding day when you can go and learn about bird calls. Have fun listening to one of nature's sweetest sounds!

• MOTHER NATURE'S RECORDING STUDIO •

It's a great big world and it's buzzing with sound! How about getting some of that sound down on tape? Borrow a tape recorder or camcorder, and head for the great outdoors to record bees buzzing, brooks babbling, dogs barking, birds chirping, and any of nature's sounds. You and Ma may just come up with something great!

Peep, Squirrel!

Peep, Squirrel! is a song and dance to make up and play. The melody is however you want to sing the words, "Yaddle yaddle deedle dum!" Act out the song with one person being a squirrel, and the other a tree. If there are more singers in your group, have more trees, but keep just one squirrel.

The squirrel scurries around the trees, acting out the song in time to the "yaddle yaddle deedle dum" — fast or sl-oooo-w. Also, it adds to the fun if you start softly and get louder. When you get to the "catch" line, the trees can move freely to tag the squirrel!

> ***Peep, Squirrel!***
>
> *Yaddle yaddle deedle dum*
>
> *Yaddle yaddle deedle dum*
>
> *Yaddle yaddle deedle dum*
>
> *Peep, Squirrel! Yaddle yaddle deedle dum!*
>
> *Yaddle yaddle deedle dum day!*

More verses to say in place of "Peep, Squirrel!":

> Scamper, Squirrel!
>
> Hop, Squirrel!
>
> Run, Squirrel!
>
> Catch that Squirrel!

• HONOR A HIGHER POWER WITH MUSIC •

A Higher Power is a power greater than any person, place, or thing. Some people call their Higher Power, God, and others have different names for it, like Jesus, Buddha, Allah, Jehovah, the Great Spirit, the Goddess, or even simply Goodness, Truth, or Love. Thinking about our Higher Power reminds us about the best of what's inside us.

No matter what you call your Higher Power, honoring it with music will keep you in touch with this important part of your life. And learning about how others honor it will only make your life richer.

AN ANCIENT FIRE CEREMONY

Since time began, people have found peace and wisdom around fire. Fire reminds us that all things change, and that we must grow and change, too. This fire ceremony has been adapted from Native Americans of the Northwest United States, and *shamans*, or holy people, from Peru, in South America. Drumming, singing, and chanting are an important part of the ceremony.

You can hold a fire ceremony in any home with a fireplace, or in a safe place outdoors. Be sure to ask a grown-up to help. Never light a fire without grown-up supervision.

Singing drums

The ceremony begins with a prayer inviting the four winds, South, West, North, and East. The person saying the prayers faces each direction as she chants:

Oh, Winds of the South, blow upon us tonight.

Come to us, Spirit of the Serpent who reminds us by her shedding skin that we must grow and change.

•

Oh, Winds of the West, warm winds

Blow upon us tonight.

Come to us, Spirit of the Jaguar

Teach us to be strong and true to ourselves.

•

Oh, Winds of the North, cold winds

Blow upon us tonight.

Come to us Spirit of the Horse

Teach us to be wise and patient.

Teach us to be kind to others

•

Oh, Winds of the East that bring each new day

Blow upon us tonight.

Come to us Great Eagle

Teach us to see as if from above

Teach our spirits to be creative and free.

•

Mother Earth, Father Sky

Grandfather Sun, Grandmother Moon

Bless us and all people with this fire tonight.

Now the fire is lit, and the time for talking is over. As the flames catch, the people who want to, may begin drumming or chanting. The drums of the fire ceremony are called *singing drums* because they express so much of what people feel. There are no rules about drumming at the fire. The drumming happens freely, out of people's moods.

At first, the drums are usually soft and quiet; they grow stronger with the fire. Have extra drums or shakers on hand, too, so that everyone who wants to can add to the beat.

The drums seem to work magic as they come together in a free-form rhythm. They call to the fire, to the Great Spirit, and to each other. Let them play or be silent, and play again.

Chant to the Great Spirit

This chant honors the spirit of our beautiful planet Earth, and of the whole Universe.

Oh, Great Spirit

Earth, sun, sky, and sea

You are inside

And all around me

To find a melody for the chant, take the words slowly. You can count out the words with this steady 1-2-3-4 beat, if you like, like this:

Oh,	Great	Spirit,	Earth	Sun	Sky	and	Sea
1-2-3-	4	1-2-3-4	1	2	3	4	1-2-3-4

You	are	in-	side	and	all around	me
1-2-3	4	1-2-3-	4	1-2-3-4-	1-2-3-	4

A private moment at the fire

Once the fire is blazing, and the drums are beating steadily, anyone who wants can go closer to it, one at a time, to take a private moment with it. Use this time for a silent prayer or private thought, or just to gaze at the beauty of the flames. If there is something you want to change, like a sad or angry feeling, you may want to write it on a piece of paper and throw it into the fire.

Ending the ceremony: A medicine circle

The end of the fire ceremony comes after the private moments at the fire. Now, the people at the ceremony become a medicine circle, sending healing thoughts or prayers into the world. People offer thoughts or prayers for other people and for peace. ("I send these thoughts for good health to my grandmother.") You can send thoughts about under-standing and guidance. You can think about whatever is good in the world.

MUSICAL JOYS

A Rainy Day Special: The Living Room Lounge

It's pouring. The sky is dark and gray. There's no place to go, and not much to play.

We had a day like that. We were looking out the window, saying, "Yuck." Feeling stuck. Until we met a kid who knew how to make things happen — with music!

"Let's open up a dance lounge, right here in the living room!" he said, rushing to the radio. "Move the coffee table! Go get flashlights! We need strobes!"

Five minutes later, the lights were off and the volume was on. We were up on our feet, grooving to the best dance music the radio could beat. We were letting off steam, dancing like a team, feeling good inside — feeling alive.

The doorbell rang. It was Gram. "Come on in, and help us jam." Soon her hips were wiggling and she was shaking her tail. She was singing out loud; she was letting it wail.

The doorbell rang. The neighbors came in. "Hey, what's going on here? Some kind of gym?"

It didn't take long for them to loosen up their spines. "Hey, this is really fun! We should do this all the time!"

So if today is gray and wet, don't be discouraged. It's not over yet. You can clear a space for a *Living Room Lounge*. Wave your flashlights and wiggle around! Turn up the music, and groove to the sound!

CELEBRATE YOURSELF IN SONG

How about making up a special song about that very special someone you see in the mirror everyday? Oh, come on, don't be shy. Just think of all the wonderful things about you that can be put to music. All you'll need are some rhymes to match the sounds in your name, and you're on your way.

How many words can you find that make a rhyme with your name? Remember, in a song you can cheat a little when you're making up rhymes. For instance, you can say, "I'm Jeremy, ever hear a' me?" and it will pass for a rhyme.

If your name doesn't have any rhymes to go with it, put the name in the beginning of the line, like this:

I, (your name), I'm a wonderful thing

I know how to swim, I know how to sing!

I know how to dance, and how to walk the dog

Yes, I (your name) can do it all!

When you make up a song about yourself, don't be modest. It's strange, but you can brag in music and it's just fine. So why not pull out all the stops, and sing about how terrific you really are? Chances are the results will be funny and charming. And just think, if you're ever feeling blue, you'll have the perfect song to lift your spirits!

• LIP SYNCHING •

It's flamboyant! It's fantastic! It's phenomenal! It's you being a brilliant artist, a celebrity, a giant talent — and more! Lip synching (SINK-ing) brings out the superstar in everyone!

When you lip synch, you play a CD, record, or tape of a great singer doing his or her thing. Then, you move your lips to match the sound so it *seems* like you're the one singing.

Hey, it's not as easy as it sounds, but guess what? It's even more fun!

Choose an artist to imitate

When you choose the song you want to lip synch, pick one that displays real vocal talent and emotion. Elvis Presley, Barbra Streisand, Neil Diamond, Whitney Houston, Mick Jagger, Oscar the Grouch, Raffi, or Sharon, Lois, and Bram — the artists you choose are up to you.

Team up with a family member or friend to do musical groups. If you've picked a song with instrumental solos, they can be pantomimed, too, as in playing the "air guitar." If you want to get really fancy, you can make cardboard cutout musical instrument shapes to hold. Also, if you're a girl who wants to do Elvis, no problem. In lip synching, anything goes.

Now, along with mouthing the words, great lip synchers also get into the movements that go with the song — moving their bodies, outstretching their arms, clenching their fists — all to add to the dramatic effect of the song's presentation. Remember, while lip synching, you *become* the artists for a brief moment of great fun and high drama!

Make a mike

A small flashlight makes a great microphone for a lip syncher in concert, and so does the dog's toy ice cream cone. The cardboard tube from a paper towel roll will do, too. Bread sticks or pretzel sticks are really good mikes because you can eat them at the end of the song. That always gets a laugh.

If you haven't got any of these things handy, make a mike with a piece of construction paper. Just roll it up the long way, fold it over, and staple the inside of the bottom. Draw a mesh pattern on the top third of the paper for an authentic studio look.

A nice added detail is a wire that can be stapled to the bottom. If you have some old stereo wire laying around, great, but a long piece of yarn or string will do just as well. The wire can add to the dramatic effect. If you've seen singers on TV, you know how they move with the mike and toss the wire out of the way from time to time. You can tug on the wire when the song reaches an emotional height, or even pretend to trip over it from time to time for a good laugh.

Know your material

It helps to be familiar with the song you're lip synching. That way you can really put on a show — the more dramatic the better. Let your face tell the story of the song. If it's a sad song (great for lip synching), don't be afraid to squeeze your eyes shut as if you have a terrible headache. Bite your lip (or the bread stick) in between phrases of the song, as you gaze out longingly over the audience's heads. When you smile, let it be a smile that would melt Antarctica.

Try to mouth the words of the song carefully, and remember to open your mouth really wide on the big notes.

Lip synching is such a hoot that you can do it all by yourself, just for fun! Try it in front of a mirror if you don't believe us. You'll see!

CONSTRUCTION PAPER

ROLL IT UP LONG WAYS

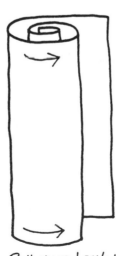

FOLD IN HALF
AND STAPLE
INSIDE BOTTOM

STAPLE YARN
TO BOTTOM
FOR WIRE

DRAW → MESH PATTERN ON TOP

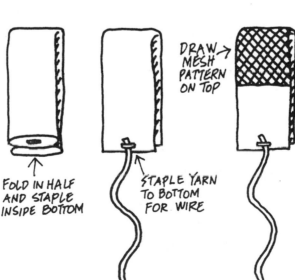

• A LITTLE TRAVELING MUSIC •

A quiet car concert

If you've ever taken a long trip in a car, you know that music can help make the time fly by. Just listening to music on the radio or portable tape or CD player makes traveling more fun.

But did you know you can make music right in the back seat of a car without driving the driver to distraction? We're talking about a *Quiet Car Concert*.

All you need are rubber bands, string, and a paper cup or two. You can make a quiet violin by tying the string and threading it through the bottom of the cup. As you pluck the string, quiet sounds will come out — high or low, depending on how tight and short the string is held.

The driver may not be able to appreciate the sounds of your hand-made violin, but if you hold your ear to the cup, you will. Wow! Close up, your quiet concert won't be quiet at all!

Paper cup guitars aren't quite as quiet, but almost. If you have a traveling companion in the back seat, sit close enough to hear each other's vibrations, and you can play your instruments together.

Tap dancing fingers

If you've got a pair of old gloves to spare, make a set of tap dancing fingertips! This instrument can travel with you, too. It's just the right sound level for taking on car trips, played on a hard-covered book.

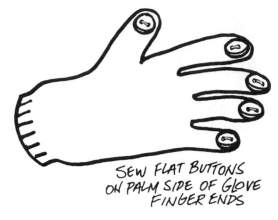

SEW FLAT BUTTONS ON PALM SIDE OF GLOVE FINGER ENDS

To make your fingertip tapper, sew buttons onto the end of the glove fingers. Presto! Every one of your fingers has just become a little drum!

Traveling tambourine

Take a few coins and jingle them in your hand. You'll have yourself a tambourine you can really count on!

• GO TO A CONCERT •

If you've never been to a *concert*, are you ever in for a treat! A concert is a chance to hear musicians playing the music they know best. There are rock concerts for rock 'n' roll fans, folk concerts for people who love folk music, and classical music concerts for people who want to hear classical music. People who go to concerts even dress differently for the different kinds of music they're going to listen to. Folk music fans tend to dress casually, while classical music fans usually get dressed up.

You can find out what concerts are coming up in your area by checking the entertainment section of the newspaper. Your music teacher at school will probably know about the music scene in your area, too, and will be happy to help in finding a concert to go to.

Free concerts are usually advertised on library bulletin boards. There are usually a lot of free concerts in the summer when they can be held in parks outdoors, and also at holiday time, when schools and community choruses and orchestras like to perform. Ask a grown-up to take you to one.

Be sure to arrive early enough to get a good seat, in case there is open seating, which is first come, first served. During the performance, sit back, turn on your imagination, and enjoy. The only rule is "No Talking, Please" — at a concert, it's the musicians who get to put out all the sounds!

At folk and rock concerts, you can show your appreciation by clapping along with the music. But at a classical concert, save your reaction for the end — even if the musicians take occasional pauses during their performances. (Pauses during classical concerts often are for movements, or sections, of symphonies. Applause during the pauses might break the mood of the serious music.) But at the end of a classical concert, clap as hard as you wish. You can even stand up and shout, "Bravo!" if you think the music was absolutely wonderful!

Of course, if you're going to a concert — or even if you're just listening to music at home, it helps to know a little bit about how those magnificent sounds are made!

• FAMOUS INSTRUMENT FAMILIES •

Instruments are a little like people — and not just because they are noisy, either. They also come in families, like we do.

Here is an album of some famous musical instrument families. Look for them at concerts and listen for them on recordings.

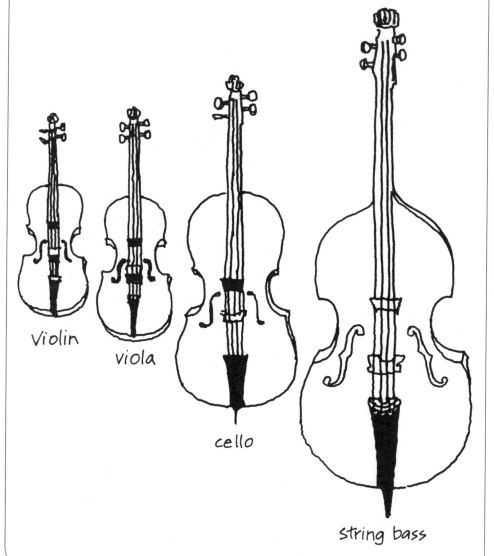

Violin

viola

cello

string bass

Meet the Strings

This is *Violin* — his nickname is Fiddle. He's the smallest in the String family, but one of the most talented. He can make sweet sounds that seem to float in the air. But he likes to play country music, and even jazz, too.

Viola is Violin's big sister. She makes a deeper sound than Violin, and is also terribly talented. She doesn't often play country music, though. She prefers classical music, like her mother, Ms. Cello.

Ms. *Cello* is Violin and Viola's mother. She's so big that she stands on the floor when being played. Her tone is deep, but mellow and rich. When she plays, there's a soothing, warm quality to her sound.

Mr. *String Bass* (pronounced "base") is the largest member of the String family. His low-toned boom makes an excellent timekeeper for any group of instruments. And talk about versatile! He's as comfortable playing jazz as he is in a country band or in a classical orchestra!

The Strings have a country cousin called *Guitar.* She's fantastic at folk music, like her brother *Banjo,* who only plays folk. But Guitar is a talented classical music maker, too.

And let's not forget Lady *Harp,* one of the loveliest strings. Her sounds are so heavenly that people imagine angels playing her! She doesn't appear very often, but when she does, she's always a star!

Say "Hi" to the Woodwinds

Ms. *Flute* knows her ancestors were once made of wood — that's how she got the name woodwind. But for the past hundred years or so, she's been made from silver, nickel, or gold. Ms. Flute makes music like a bird, trilling out a most pleasant sound. She's very popular in the orchestra and the band.

Ms. Flute's baby, Little *Piccolo*, makes the same trilling sounds as his mother, but he makes them much higher. He loves to have fun with harmonies in the orchestra and to be in marching bands, but is too shy to play jazz.

You won't find Aunt *Oboe* and Uncle *Bassoon* in any marching, jazz, or country bands. These two woodwinds are far too serious for that. They lend their distinctive sounds exclusively to orchestras.

bassoon

oboe

Mr. *Saxophone* is another woodwind who's made from brass. (So much for the "wood" in the woodwind name.) Sax, as his pals call him, plays all sorts of music, from military marches to classical concerts, but his real love is jazz. His smooth, sultry tone is right at home in a jazz club, where he can really let it wail.

Cousin *Clarinet* is as comfortable on the marching field, as he is cutting up in a jazz band, or playing his part in a classical orchestra. He's good at letting his music out freely, improvising as he goes along, too!

Hold on to your ears! The Horns are here!

There's nothing shy or subtle about these two. *Trumpet* and *Cornet* like to let their music blare full out! They make their big brassy sounds wherever and whenever they can, too. If you listen, you'll hear them in orchestras, jazz bands, and on the football field. They love to be a part of Hispanic music, too. Listen for them on a Spanish radio station and you'll see what we mean.

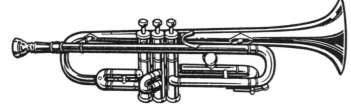

Monsieur *French Horn*, like the Oboe and Bassoon, is most at home in a classical orchestra. Sometimes, he remembers his hunting ancestors, who called to hunters over hill and dale. But that is all history now as he lends his rich, mellow tone to the most sophisticated music around.

Watch our for Tom the *Trombone*! His long elbow slides out and is called a "crook." Not only that, this guy can get in anybody's way! But what a sound he makes — long, low, and moaning. He's a main feature in any parade and on the marching field, and he does well in orchestras, too.

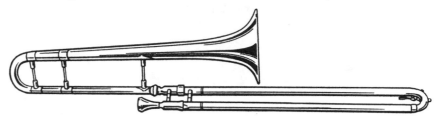

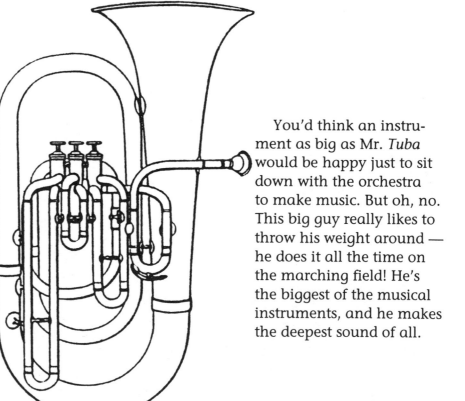

You'd think an instrument as big as Mr. *Tuba* would be happy just to sit down with the orchestra to make music. But oh, no. This big guy really likes to throw his weight around — he does it all the time on the marching field! He's the biggest of the musical instruments, and he makes the deepest sound of all.

The Pounding Percussions

Grandma and Grandpa *Piano* play everything, everywhere! Jazz, country, pop, rock, show tunes, and classical — pianos play it all! Why are pianos so versatile and special? Maybe it's because they can play a melody and a beat at the same time! All a human has to do is add the feelings!

Timpani have another name, too — *kettledrums*. These big babies like to be beaten, banged, and biffed. They sit in the back of the orchestra, biding their time until the big moment when they wake the audience up with their powerful booms!

The *Cymbal* twins are never really far apart — we guess they'd be too lonely — for cymbals always come in pairs. Their specialty is crashing together dramatically at the high point of the music. They like to play in marching bands, too.

Peter and the Wolf

If you would like to hear some of these instruments, borrow *Peter and the Wolf*, by Serge Prokofiev, from the library. In that musical tale about a boy who saves a bird, different instruments stand for each character. A narrator guides you through the story.

For Peter, it's a *string quartet*, four stringed instruments playing together. The bird is played by a *flute*, the duck by an *oboe*, the cat by a *bass clarinet*, which is a clarinet that plays in a lower tone than the more common kind. Peter's grandfather is represented by a *bassoon*, the wolf by three *horns*, and hunters by *kettledrums* and *bassdrums*.

Every time you hear one of these instruments, it is very much like the character walking on stage in a play.

Instruments in the airwaves

Once you know the sound of the different instruments, it's fun to pick them out when you listen to music.

Turn on the radio, a CD or tape player, and listen. How many instruments can you identify? The more you listen, the better you'll get at identifying what is playing when. Start simply by choosing one instrument to listen for, like the violin. Then, add on, listening for violin and drums; then, violin, drums, and flute, and so on. Soon you'll know all of the instruments as individuals!

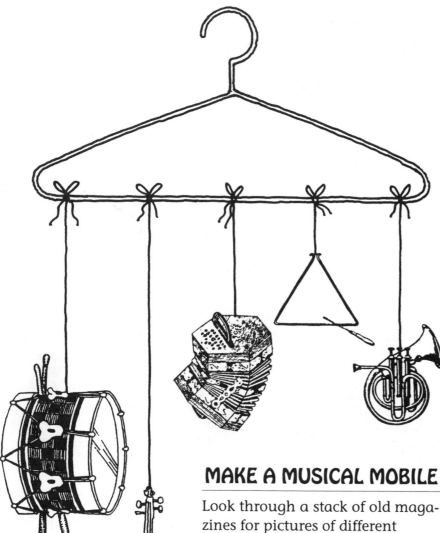

MAKE A MUSICAL MOBILE

Look through a stack of old magazines for pictures of different musical instruments to cut out. Or, draw the instruments on cardboard, and paint them bright, fanciful colors with tempera paint. Then, poke holes near the tops. Thread string or yarn through the holes, and tie onto a wire hanger. Presto! An instant orchestra!

• OLD MACDONALD HAD AN ORCHESTRA •

That Old MacDonald was a busy guy! He didn't just have a farm with mooing cows, oinking pigs, and quacking ducks. He also had an orchestra with all sorts of musical instruments. Can you think of more than we did? Pretend to play the instruments as you sing about them.

Old MacDonald had an orchestra, E-I-E-I-O

And in that orchestra he had a flute, E-I-E-I-O

With a toodle oodle here, and a toodle oodle there

Here a toodle

There an oodle

Everywhere a toodle oodle

Old MacDonald had an orchestra

E-I-E-I-O!

Trumpet: braaaam braaaam
Tuba: (low) oo oo
Piano: plink plink plinkety plink
Guitar: strum strum
Drum: boom boom
Cymbal: crash crash
Bass: bum, bah, bum

STREET RHYMES

Street rhymes are good for counting out turns, jump rope, and ball bouncing. The best thing about them, though, is that they're kid-created! These rhythmic rhymes have been passed from kid to kid down through the ages — which is why they're so much fun!

Make up any tune you like to these. Afterall, as a kid, *you* are the expert here! Then, grab a jump rope or a ball and set up a rhythm you can jump or bounce to — fast is more difficult!

Miss Lucy

Miss Lucy had a baby; she called him Tiny Tim.

She put him in the bathtub to see if he could swim.

He drank up all the water. He ate up all the soap;

He tried to eat the bathtub, but it got caught in his throat!

•

Miss Lucy called the doctor; the doctor called the nurse;

The nurse called the lady with the alligator purse.

"Measles," said the doctor; "Mumps," said the nurse;

"Penicillin," said the lady, and put Tiny in her purse!

Old Man Moses

Old Man Moses sick in bed

He called for the doctor, the doctor said

Take two steps forward and turn yourself around

Do the wiggle waggle and get out of town!

Chant the last two lines while acting out the meaning and jumping rope or bouncing a ball.

For deciding whose turn it is, try these:

My mother and your mother

Talk every day

Every time they have a fight

This is what they say,

Ickabacker, ickabacker, ickabacker, boo!

Ickabacker, soda cracker, out goes you!

Or,

Bubble gum, bubble gum in a dish

How many pieces do you wish? (Person says a number, say, three)

Three? One, two, three, and out you go

With your mother's big fat toe!

Try this one for jumping rope:

Blondie and Dagwood went to town

Blondie bought an evening gown

Dagwood bought the Daily News

And this is what it said:

Close your eyes and count to ten

If you miss you take the end

1,2,3,4,5,6,7,8,9,10.

This is one tough Little Dutch Girl to hand jive to. Follow the hand signals as shown to get a fun way to keep the rhythm. The faster you go, the harder it gets.

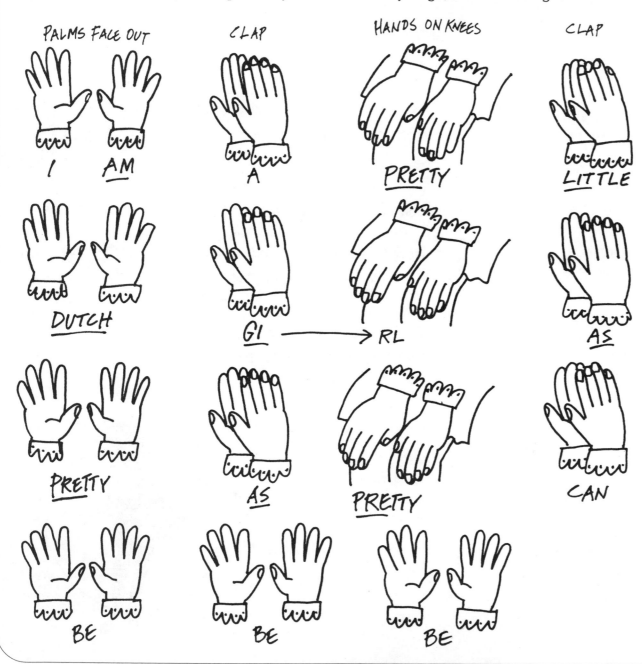

PALMS FACE OUT
I   AM

CLAP
A

HANDS ON KNEES
PRETTY

CLAP
LITTLE

DUTCH

GI ⟶ RL

AS

PRETTY

AS

PRETTY

CAN

BE

BE

BE

I am a pretty little Dutch girl
As pretty as pretty can be! Be! Be!
And all the boys around the block
Are crazy over me! Me! Me!

My boyfriend's name is Chatty
He comes from Cincinnati
With a pickle on his nose
And twenty-four toes
And here's the way my story goes

One day he gave me peaches
One day he gave me pears
One day he gave me fifty cents
And kicked me down the stairs

I gave him back his peaches
I gave him back his pears
I gave him back his fifty cents
And kicked him down the stairs!

OPEN YOUR EARS! OPEN YOUR HEART!

A magic carpet ride

Listening to good music is like stepping onto a magic carpet. It can take you far away from the ordinary world around you. It can lift you up and bring you to a new world of fantasy and wonder. The more you listen, the more that world will open up for you, too.

Different music for different moods

However you are feeling, whatever you are doing, there is music to match your mood and activity. The rock music you listen to when you clean your room is different from the soft classical music you want to hear in the background when you do homework. The rap you dance to will be different than the jazz you daydream to.

TRY SOMETHING NEW

Do you or your family have any records or CDs or tapes of music? Try playing one that you have never heard before!

Let the music filter into your body. Listen with your whole being. Let the music bounce off the walls of your brain, and flow down to your fingers and toes. Pretend that you are the one who is playing the music. Lie down, sit, stand, or dance around — it doesn't matter. Just let the music move you.

Acquired tastes

Do you eat olives? Or pickles? Or drink tea without sugar? Sometimes when people are very young those things don't taste good to them. But after time goes by, the person tries them again and wow! She likes them! That's called an acquired taste.

It's the same with music. You may not like classical music or jazz the first time you hear it. But give yourself time. Some music has to grow on you. Check in with different kinds of sounds every so often. You may be surprised at the discoveries you make — about the music and, most importantly, about your musical self!

• EXPLORE! •

In the world of classical music, try listening to pieces composed by Bach, Mozart, Beethoven, Tchaikovsky, Stravinsky, Schubert, Satie, Debussy, or Dvorak. Each has a different way of expressing the same feelings that we humans all have. Which is your favorite?

Bach's *Air On a G String* is a great starter. As you close your eyes and listen, imagine yourself floating in the air, gliding on the breeze, or diving underwater among the coral reefs. Imagining is a big key to learning to love music.

Or try Mozart's *40th Symphony*, or Beethoven's *Fifth Symphony*. Your mind's eye may conjure up colors, patterns, or shapes as the music flows in and through you, too. Ask yourself: Which feelings was the composer trying to express when he wrote the piece?

A music-inspired gingerbread house!
Here's a delicious way to learn music appreciation. Find a copy of the opera, *Hansel and Gretel*, by classical composer Englebert Humperdink. (It's probably at your local library.) As you listen to it, make — and eat — a gingerbread house!

Construct the walls from graham crackers, using cream cheese mixed with a little milk for mortar. Place thin cookies, or wafers, on the roof for shingles, stick on some Life Saver™ windows to give the house a fancier look. A border of gum drops adds color — and flavor, too.

• PAINT A SONG •

Music can inspire great art! Find out by drawing or painting to music. First, gather your art supplies, and get ready to create. Then pick out some music to paint or draw to. Choose different kinds, some fast, some slow, some classical, and some rock 'n' roll. Label each piece of paper with the kind of music you'll be listening to while you draw.

Now put the first kind of music on, and listen. Let yourself get a feel for the music, then let the music guide your hand and imagination. Does this type of music inspire you to use certain colors? Which designs feel right for this music? Remember, you don't have to draw any particular "thing" — just give your hand the freedom to respond to the music.

When you have at least three different drawings, examine your creations. Do they look like the music that inspired them? Show them to other people. Can they guess which kind of music they match?

Mussorgsky's *Pictures at an Exhibition* is a musical story that takes the listener through a gallery of fascinating paintings. In real life, the music was a tribute to the art of Victor Hartemann who was Mussorgsky's friend.

The music begins with a walk — or promenade — through an art gallery. The first painting is of a gnome; then comes one of an Italian landscape, followed by a picture of children playing (and quarrelling) in the brisk morning air. Next is a painting of an ox cart; then chicks in their shells, and then, a rich and poor man talking together. Then, comes a painting of a busy marketplace.

Find the music at the library and draw as it plays. You can create your own gallery of art work — to music!

WHAT'S YOUR STYLE?

Music has a long history and styles of music have changed over time, just like styles of clothes. Over the centuries people found different ways to express those basic human feelings that we all have.

So what's your style? Read on, and we think you'll find there's lots to like in all different kinds of music. More importantly, *listen* to a lot of different music. The more you come to know it, the more you might come to love it — or not! But at least you will have given it a chance. And who knows? You may even change your mind at some point in your life.

THE BEATLES FOREVER

• CLASSICAL MUSIC •

Classical music is music that has lasted for years and years. When you see the words, "Classical music," written with a capital "C," it means music written from 1750 to 1820, during the *Classical Period.* When you see classical music, with a little "c," it means any serious music that's played in a *concert hall* or place where people go to listen to music.

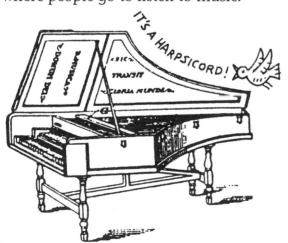

Capital "C" musicians

Mozart, Haydn, Schubert, Bach, and Beethoven are some of the most famous capital "C" Classical musicians. Their music is astounding! They wrote for *orchestras,* or bands with many kinds of instruments. They wrote short pieces called *sonatas,* and large pieces of music, called *symphonies.* They also wrote *concertos,* for an orchestra and one "solo" player. The idea of a concerto is to show off the talent of a particular player (see *Toothbrush Concerto,* page 15).

The Classical music that the capital "C" musicians wrote is still very much with us today. You can hear it playing all over the world, every place from restaurants to concert halls to elevators!

Not too serious, though

Even though Classical music is serious, it doesn't mean the Classical musicians didn't like a good joke now and then. Some of their symphonies are really sym*funnys.* Your library probably has a copy of *The Toy Symphony* by Leopold Mozart, the father of the more famous Wolfgang Amadeus Mozart. He wrote that one to make people laugh.

Composer of the week

Here's a great way to get acquainted with the Classical musicians. Write down their names on separate slips of paper and put them in a hat. Then, every week, pick one out of the hat to celebrate as "Composer of the Week."

Take some of his music out of the library, or off the shelf, and get to know it. Put on a record, tape, or CD while you're doing your homework, or just hanging around the house. You might want to take out a book about the composer's life from the library, or look him up in an encyclopedia, too. It's fascinating to see how the composer's life affected the music he created.

Perhaps you'll want to make a time line of a group of composers' lives and important events that happened while they were composing. You can decorate it with pictures cut out of magazines or that you draw, so you'll have a visual image of their lives.

Plan some fun around your Composer of the Week, too. How about a *Mozart Macaroni Party*, where you eat different kinds of pasta with Mozart's music playing in the background?

Or, try a game of *Haydn Seek*, playing while Haydn's music plays! How about *Bach Around the Clock*, playing Bach when you first get up and again before bed? Or a *Bopping Beethoven Pillow Fight*? Ba ba ba BOOM!

Does this sound familiar?

Read this out loud: Bah Bah Bah BUM
Bah Bah Bah BUM

Congratulations! You've just done the first notes of Beethoven's famous *Fifth Symphony*. It's strong stuff — solid, passionate, and angry! Without words, and using just eight notes, Beethoven managed to "say" something that people still understand today. That's the power of great classical music.

Put on the *Fifth* and "bah, bah, bah, bum" your way through this world famous symphony. You'll find the rest of it as exciting as that first phrase.

GETTING STARTED WITH THE CLASSICS

So this classical stuff sounds pretty good to you, but now what? Well, there really is a lot of classical music out there and sometimes it is nice to know where to get started listening — just like you know where your favorite kinds of books are located in the library.

Here's a list of music that you might enjoy as you explore classical music. If one doesn't strike your musical self, then just move onto another one, until you find what is right for you.

Pachabel's *Canon in D Major*
Stravinsky's *The Firebird*
Beethoven's *Fifth Symphony*
Haydn's *Surprise Symphony*
Tchaikovsky's *Nutcracker Suite*
Bach's *Brandenburg Concerti*
Berlioz's *Symphony Fantastique*
Satie — any of his works

• CONDUCT A CLASSIC •

Find a record, tape, or CD of one of the Classical musicians. Then get ready to conduct an imaginary orchestra!

Make sure you have plenty of room — you'll need it for conducting! You'll also need a baton; all conductors do. A chopstick or long pencil will do perfectly, and so will a pointed finger.

Now, pretend you're standing in front of a giant orchestra. All eyes are on you! Behind you the audience waits expectantly. In front of you, the musicians look to you to guide them through the music, keep the time, and make sure they play together. It's a big job, but you can do it!

Give a confident, dignified nod, first to the audience, then to your musicians. Then shake out your hair — the wilder the better — raise your arms, and GO! When the music begins, start keeping time. Let the music work on you. Listen, and respond to the feelings it's trying to communicate. Get carried away! Get wild!

ALUMINUM FOIL
CHOPSTICK
ROLL CHOPSTICK IN FOIL
PAINT WITH GOLD

MAKE A SILVER OR GOLD BATON

For a silver baton, roll a chopstick up in aluminum foil. For a gold one, paint the chopstick with shiny gold paint — the kind you can buy at a hobby shop. Be sure to tap the baton on a music stand or table to get your orchestra's attention before the music begins. Then, you're off and running to the beat and flow of the music, waving your sparkling baton high in the air, or gently in front of you to keep the orchestra together!

CONDUCTING SHAPES

Real conductors use their right hand to keep the basic beat of the song. They make certain patterns in the air with their batons that help the orchestra keep the beat.

Trace these patterns in the air with a baton or your fingertip, and you'll be keeping time just like a real conductor does!

For 1-2 time (clap, clap):

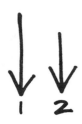

For 1-2-3-4 time (clap, clap, clap, clap):

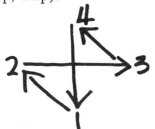

For 1-2-3 time (clap, clap, clap):

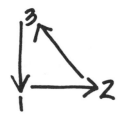

Use your left hand to introduce, or "cue," new instruments, or let it wave around, expressing itself. If you want the orchestra to play more softly, say so with your left hand, by patting the air in a downward motion. If you want it louder, raise your hand with palm to the ceiling.

As you conduct, notice how parts of the music get played, and played again, twisting around and changing, until they come back to the first way you heard them. Those are *themes* — and as the conductor, you're the one who makes sure they're heard!

Playing conductor is a great way to get acquainted with classical music. And who knows — someday, you may become a real conductor! If you do, you're likely to be around for a long time — because of all the jobs and professions, conductors live the longest! Maybe it's because they spend their lives expressing their feelings in such an active way!

OPERA AND OPERETTAS

Sometime around the 1700s, someone got the bright idea of combining Classical music with theater. That's how opera — a story told only in song — was born!

In the beginning, opera was very serious, performed only for the rich and the royal. Then some bright composer decided to make it easier for other people to understand. He took a light-hearted play and put it to music. People loved going to see musical plays with dancing and fun. And so a new art form was created, a smashing success, called operetta!

Johann Strauss's *The Bat* (also called *Der Fledermaus*) and Gilbert and Sullivan's *Pirates of Penzance* are two famous operettas that you may like. *The Sorcerer's Apprentice* and *Amal and the Night Visitors* are operas you may like, too.

• THERE'S NO BUSINESS LIKE SHOW BUSINESS — AND NO MUSIC LIKE SHOW MUSIC •

Have you ever heard of *My Fair Lady, South Pacific, Oklahoma!, West Side Story, Fiddler on the Roof* or *The King and I*? How about *Guys and Dolls, Annie Get Your Gun, A Chorus Line* or *Grease*? If you haven't, you're in for a treat! Those are names of famous *Broadway musicals* — plays with music and dancing that have thrilled millions of people all over the world. *The difference between a musical and an operetta is that musicals have more parts that are spoken, and operettas are almost all in song.*

Oklahoma! was the first musical to have a real, developed story line that fit right in with the music. It was written by Richard Rodgers and Oscar Hammerstein. It featured dancing cowboys and people singing about the windswept plains of a brand new state. When *Oklahoma!* opened on Broadway back in the 1940s, it created a sensation! The audience realized that a new art form was being introduced — one that would dazzle and delight people for years to come.

We are sure that you can get recordings of any of the shows we mentioned from the library. Lots of Broadway musicals have been made into movies that you can rent, too. Give yourself a treat! Listen to a Broadway musical soon! (And if listening and watching gets your energy flowing, maybe you and your neighbors or classmates can stage your own adaptation of your favorite musical. It's lots of fun.)

Let's Go!

Lots of times, touring acting companies come to small towns and cities presenting musicals that were once on Broadway. Sometimes they even have special children's performances that your class can attend. Why not ask your teacher or a grown-up if any shows ever come near to where you live? Maybe you could help organize a class trip or a family outing.

Be a choreographer

A *choreographer* (cory-OG-raffer) is a person who creates dances. If you borrow a recording of a musical from the library, you can be a choreographer, too! Listen for a song you like — preferably one with a fast tempo — and then make up a dance to go with it.

Every song in a musical tells a story. Let your dance tell the story of the song you've picked.

If you pick the song *One Singular Sensation* from *A Chorus Line*, use your top hat and cane in the dance (see *Tap Dancing*, page 52). If you pick the title song from *Oklahoma!*, pretend you are a cowboy, riding up the windy plain. If you pick *I'm Gonna Wash That Man Right Out of My Hair* from *South Pacific*, pretend you are washing your hair as you dance.

The only rule for making up dances to show tunes is to give it your all! If you do that, your dance is sure to be dazzling!

SOME UNSUNG GREATS (HA!) OF MUSIC: FROM PRE-HISTORY TO THE MIDDLE AGES

Ugg the Caveman, born 10,003 B.C.

When Ugg discovered that all the berries near his cave had been eaten by a group of nomads, he got so mad that he started banging rocks together. Soon, he forgot his rage and started grooving to the beat! Scholars now hail Ugg as the great-grand-ancestor of rhythm!

Irma the Tribeswoman, born 6,000 B.C.

Irma had nine kids who wandered over hill and valley, looking for roots to dig and eat. One night at dusk, instead of shouting for them to come home, Irma picked up a ram's horn and blew into it. The fearsome blast sent her kids running home. Irma is now credited with the development of the horn.

Raba the Archer, born 3,024 B.C.

Raba the Archer felt horrible when he lost his girlfriend, Sha Na Na, to another guy who'd offered her a fatter water buffalo as a wedding gift. Feeling quite forlorn, Raba reached down and plucked his bow string as he let out a sad sigh. The pleasant sound soon made him forget his sadness. When the Pharaoh heard it, he offered Raba a job as his court musician!

Frank the Monk, born 1,011 A.D.

Frank's job in the monastery was getting the local serfs and oafs to sing on key when they came to church. The trouble was that notes, scales, and keys hadn't been invented. So Frank invented them, bringing heavenly sounds to the Middle Ages.

Robin the Troubadour, born 1206 A.D.

Robin was a busybody who loved to travel from town to town gossiping about other people's loves and lives. But nobody was interested until she picked up a lute and began singing her stories. With music, her tales became fascinating ballads. Suddenly, everyone wanted to hear what Robin had to say!

• FOLK MUSIC •

Folk music is music that belongs to everyone! It's the do-it-yourself music of everyday people — songs that have been sung for hundreds of years.

Most folk music was made up by people whose names are long forgotten, though their tunes live on. You can even think of it as recycled music, because in folk music the same tunes have been used by different people at different times in different places to tell about their different ways of life!

But even though folk music has been around for ages, the best thing about it is that it's still being created! As long as there is music in people's hearts, there will be new folk music. In fact, this is one kind of music that has to be created again and again and again!

In other words, folk music needs *you*!

Do-It-Yourself: Skip to My Lou

This song is fun to sing and act out. It has lots of verses, but it can still use more. Maybe you'll make up a new one! When you act out the song, think about the old-fashioned farm life it describes. Then try making up a verse that describes the kind of life you lead!

To get you started, here are some more words that rhyme with Lou: chew, flew, Sue, new, boo, due, do, who, clue, true, glue, and tofu! Or, give Lou another name, if you want to use other rhymes.

Skip, skip, skip to my Lou
Skip, skip, skip to my Lou
Skip, skip, skip to my Lou
Skip to my Lou, my darling!

Chicks in the garden, shoo chicks shoo!
Chicks in the garden, shoo chicks shoo!
Chicks in the garden, shoo chicks shoo!
Skip to my Lou, my darling!

Pigs in the parlor, shoo, pigs, shoo
Pigs in the parlor, shoo, pigs, shoo
Pigs in the parlor, shoo, pigs, shoo
Skip to my Lou, my darling!

Now make up some verses about your life! Here's one to get you started:

Went to the mall, the mall was new
Went to the mall, the mall was new
Sat in the food court and ate tofu
Skip to my Lou, my darling!

Living history

Folk music is like a living history book, too. If you're interested in a particular period of history, there's sure to be folk music to go with it. Here are some folk songs that tell about the building of America. Ask someone to teach them to you, or borrow a recording of them from the library.

I've Been Working on the Railroad

This Old Hammer (about building the railroad)

Sweet Betsy from Pike (about pioneers going west)

Darlin' Clementine (about the Gold Rush)

These songs were written at the time of the Civil War.

Glory, Glory Hallelujah

Dixie

When Johnny Comes Marching Home

This Old Hammer

Before railroads, the only way to get goods across the country was to carry them on a horse!

When workers first laid the tracks that would bring the country together, they worked with hammers. When you're singing this song, listen for where the hammer would bang, and act the song out. Make up the melody if you can't find someone who knows it.

This old hammer

Shines like silver

Shines like gold, boys,

Shines like gold

Well, don't you hear that

Hammer ringing?

Drivin' steel, boys,

Drivin' steel

Ain't no hammer

On this mountain

Rings like mine, boys,

Rings like mine

Greensleeves

Did you know that the famous ballad *Greensleeves* was written by King Henry VIII of England, for his wife, Anne Boleyn? The name of the song comes from the custom of the day for ladies to wear the colors of the knight they loved on their sleeves when the knights were jousting.

The king was a talented composer, all right, but he also had his down-side — namely, a very nasty temper. When old Henry got mad at Anne, he had her head chopped off!

Alas, true love doesn't always last as long as a good song!

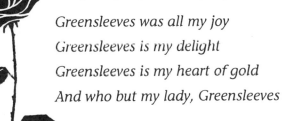

Greensleeves

Alas, my love, you do me wrong

To treat me so discourteously

And I have lov-ed you so long

Delighting in your company

Greensleeves was all my joy

Greensleeves is my delight

Greensleeves is my heart of gold

And who but my lady, Greensleeves

BE A TROUBADOUR

Troubadours were folk musicians from days of old who told about the events of people's lives in song. They wandered from town to town singing about what was happening elsewhere. In fact, troubadours were sort of like singing newspapers.

If you know an event that is soon coming, you can tell about it in song, too. Did your aunt recently become engaged to marry? You can celebrate the news in song! Is your Scout troop going to have a picnic? Announce it with a ballad!

Remember, every song needs a feeling along with a beat and a melody. Ask yourself how you feel about the event. If you feel sad that your aunt will be moving away, put that in the ballad you create. If you're looking forward to the picnic, but worried about the ants and mosquitoes coming to it, add a line about that, too. Here are some ideas to help you get started as a troubadour.

The Scouts' Picnic

On June the 12th, next Saturday
All ye Scouts come out and play
For if the weather is not ick
There will be a Scout picnic!

So gather all ye Scouts at ten
In front of Ms. Harley's den
And be sure to wear long pants
In case we meet a troop of ants!

A Wedding Announcement

She has been known as Miss Jenny King,
But that all changed with her diamond ring
And come September twenty-two
A bride she'll be of Mr. Wu!

Aunt Jenny then will start to roam
She'll make Vancouver her new home
And though we know we'll miss her so
We also know she has to go!

So go with our love, Aunt Jenny, our own
But do not forget to pick up the phone!
And as for Wu since you love him,
We'll give him a try as Uncle Jim!

Songs from the old country

Where did your ancestors come from? There are lots of folk songs from different lands, telling about what life was like there. With a little digging, you're sure to come up with some good examples from your ancestors' "old country." Ask a parent or grandparent or older neighbor, if they know any songs from their "old country."

Folk music belongs to everybody. And now, it belongs to you, too.

• SOMETHING SPECIAL — JAZZ! •

Jazz is cool, and jazz is hot. Jazz is one-of-a-kind music, totally unique. Jazz is music that's made up just for fun. It's an American language that's understood all over the world. Jazz is a free-form, moving, shaking, improvised, musical force that takes its listeners to a whole, other place.

How it all started

Some say jazz was invented by a newsboy called Stale Bread, who picked up a dishpan and played it for a drum. Others say it came from a kid name Jasper who played with a band called Spasm Band, because of the way it made people dance. Others say jazz was named for Charles, a horn player who wrote his name, Chaz. The truth is a lot of people helped create this unique American music, because the heart and soul of jazz is making up music — on the spot.

• A CITY THAT JUMPED •

Jazz first came to be in New Orleans around 1900. In those days, music making was a big part of everybody's life. There was no TV, so on weekends, music makers would gather on street corners, crooning and wailing for people passing by.

New Orleans had a place called Congo Square, too, where African-Americans came to beat out the rhythms of their ancestors. They filled the square with a rocking, rolling beat never heard in America before. When the drums started up in Congo Square, New Orleans jumped.

A rich musical history

Music makers of New Orleans had a rich musical history to draw on. Along with those strong African and Caribbean beats were Spanish and French songs, too, because New Orleans had belonged to both France and Spain, before it became part of the United States.

Many of the poor workers of the Deep South were the sons and daughters of enslaved people, brought to the United States against their will. Their music was a tribute to the pain, and strength, inside them. They made up "field hollers" to make their hard work go easier.

• MAKE UP YOUR OWN FIELD HOLLER •

You can use field hollers to make the work you have to do easier. Next time it's your turn to wash dishes, begin tapping your toe to a strong beat and making up words something like this:

Running the water, running.

Add the soap now, add it.

Gonna swish up a dish, and shine it up right

Gonna wash these dishes till they're nice and bright.

Gonna rinse off the dish, now, rinse it!

Put it in the rack to dry.

Gonna swish off another and a whole lot more

Till the dishes are all done by and by.

Just saying the words, you begin to feel the rhythm. That's how field hollers worked — they set up a nice steady rhythm to work by.

The right recipe

By combining the African beats of their ancestors with English hymns, African-Americans created songs called *spirituals*, and a style called *gospel music*. This gospel music raised up their lives of hard work, inspiring these good people to stay in touch with higher truths.

When you take the strong African drumbeat, add a French or Spanish song for flavor, combine it all with a field holler, and cook it up with a gospel song — then you've got the music played, heard, and loved around the whole world today — *jazz*!

• SYNCOPATION •

Don't be scared by this big word! We're sure that you have heard syncopated rhythm many times, though you may not have known it by name. In *syncopation* (SINK-uh-PAY-shun), an "off beat" is stressed. Syncopation gives music extra oomph, energy, and fun.

You can think of it this way: When you walk, your feet make a regular (or *un*-syncopated) beat. When you skip, it's syncopation!

Here's another way to put it: Jumping rope makes regular rhythm, but Double Dutch makes syncopation.

Clapping syncopation

This clapping exercise will help you hear syncopation, too.

First, clap and sound out this regular beat:

1 and 2 and 3 and 4. Clap on the numbers, and say the numbers as well as the "ands," too.

Then, to hear *syncopation*, clap and sound out this beat:

1 and 2 **3** and and 4. Give the bold number some extra oomph and a tad more time.

Hear the difference? That's syncopation!

Some famous syncopated tunes

If you know the song *Shortnin' Bread*, you know syncopation. The part that goes, "call up de doctor" is pure syncopation. The "up" is the off beat that's stressed.

Another famous song is *I Got Rhythm*, which someone close by is sure to know. Here's how the first line of it goes:

(beat) Clap (beat) Clap (beat) Clap (beat) Clap
    I   *got*   *rhy-*   *thm*

(beat) Clap (beat) Clap (beat) Clap (beat) Clap
    I   *got*   *mu-*   *sic*

• THE BLUES •

The blues are one of the greatest — and simplest — musical creations of all times. It uses only three chords or forty-eight beats to communicate a whole world of feeling.

The blues were created by enslaved Africans who lived in the Deep South. Sweating in the hot sun as they labored all day, they expressed all the misery, sadness, heartbreak, strength, and hope inside them, through a jazz form called blues.

Even the saddest blues song usually has a good sense of humor behind it, though. Here's a blues lyric someone came up with over a hundred years ago:

> *I'm going down to the railroad*
>
> *And lay my head on the track*
>
> *I'm going down to the railroad*
>
> *And lay my head on the track*
>
> *But if I see the train a-coming*
>
> *I'm gonna jerk it back!*

Though some blues songs have been written down, or recorded, the words to blues songs are traditionally *improvised*. That means, the music maker makes them up on the spot. Improvising music was fun back then, and it's still fun now. It's also the easiest way to create new songs.

• WHAT ARE TWELVE BARS? •

In music, a bar is a measure of time. The basic blues bar has four beats. If you clap steadily to a count of 4, you've just clapped out a bar. Try it.

Clap	Clap	Clap	Clap
1	2	3	4

Twelve-bar blues means simply that there are twelve measures of four beats each. That makes 48 beats from start to finish. Not much mystery there, is there?

Twelve-bar blues can be sung with just clapping as a background and it sounds just fine. As long as the clapping is sure and steady, the singer's voice can easily carry the song. Try it.

Clap out a twelve-bar blues

How long are forty-eight claps? Clap them out to find out. Next time, clap out the first sixteen, snap out the next eight. Remember, nice and steady.

> Clap: 16
>
> Snap: 8
>
> Clap: 8
>
> Stomp: 4
>
> Snap: 4
>
> Clap: 4
>
> Stomp: 4

Add words, and you've just created some blues!

What kind of blues do you want to sing?

The first blues singers led lives filled with crushing poverty and despair. But singing about their hard times and broken hearts seemed to ease their troubled souls. You may not have a life as miserable as the first blues singers, but you must have some problems! Why not express them in blues form? Singing the blues has a way of freeing you from even the tamest problems.

• MAKING UP THE BLUES •

Here's an example of an improvised blues song. Make up the melody and really let it wail!

The Homework Blues

Oh, I hate homework

Oh, I hate it so bad

Yes, I hate homework

Oh, yeah, I hate it so bad

But I gotta do my homework

Or else my teacher gets mad.

When you make up words to your own blues songs, don't worry whether they fit perfectly or not. As long as you can get them in the 48 beats, it'll be fine. Many blues singers finagle their lyrics into fitting by adding moans, groans, whoas, oohs, and all kinds of exclamations. These can work for you, too.

You can make up funny blues songs for and about people you know. Do any of these titles inspire you?

Filled Hamper Blues

Burnt Toast Blues

Cat Scratched the Sofa Blues

Frozen Battery Blues

Early Bedtime Blues

Anchovy Pizza Blues . . . .

• ROCK 'N' ROLL •

Rock 'n' roll is more than a kind of music — it's a way of life! When rock first burst on the music scene back in the 1950s, it changed life on earth forever! Rock 'n' roll was a kind of revolution that freed people from the inside out by getting them grooving to the beat.

Recipe for rock 'n' roll

Take the blues and add a pinch of bee bop.

Throw in some doo-wop, like at a sock hop

Start cooking what you got, and cook it non-stop

Rock your shoulders and roll your hips.

Snap your fingers and wiggle your lips

But you won't be done 'til you throw in your soul.

You got it, babe. That's rock 'n' roll.

THE ROCK BEAT

Music becomes rock 'n' roll when it has that special rock and roll beat. To learn this basic beat, start by tapping out all the numbers and the "and" that falls between them:

1 & 2 & 3 & 4 & 1 & 2 & 3 & 4 &

Once you've got that beat down, rock and roll-ize it by putting extra stress on the 2 and 4 beats. Like this:

1 & **2** & 3 & **4** & 1 & **2** & 3 & **4** &, etc.

Can you hear the rock beat in that rhythm? Pretty cool, huh?

Rock 'n' roll triplets

Another rock 'n' roll beat — one that's a little more "bluesy" is *triplets* repeated over and over. (A triplet is three quick beats, like the word mer-ri-ly.) When you drum this beat, drum the triplets quickly, with no pauses between them.

123 123 123 123 123 123 123 123 123

A ROCK 'N' ROLL PARTY

You don't need a special occasion to have a rock 'n' roll party. You can have one for a birthday or just because it's Friday night!

What you do need is a bunch of rock songs that really move you. It's fun to choose songs from the different ages of rock, too. "Bill Haley and the Comets" was one of the first rock 'n' roll groups. If you can, try to scare up a copy of *Rock Around the Clock*, the song that first launched rock music. It's as great to listen to today as it ever was. Other early rock classics are *Blue Suede Shoes*, by the King of Rock , Elvis Presley, *Johnny Be Good*, by Chuck Berry, and *Great Balls of Fire*, by Jerry Lee Lewis.

A rock 'n' roll party is a good time for *lip synching* (see page 90). And don't forget air guitar playing, too (see page 122).

Dress like a rocker

When you get dressed for your rock 'n' roll party, you can be truly and totally outrageous.

Some rockers will dress in all black — from their shirts to their boots. Other rockers choose glitzy clothes for a more glamorous look, with armbands, wristbands, scarves, rings, belts, and vests. Check out the family hat collection, too. You might find something good there. If there's a wig in the house, definitely try it on! And, guys, if you can find a clip earring — just one — it might look too cool!

Make-up? Definitely! Male or female, if you choose all black, how about lining your eyes with black eyebrow pencil for an extra intense look? "Glam" rockers, try a dot of nontoxic glue on your cheek, sprinkled with glitter to dazzle your fans.

You can even dress down for your rock party wearing your absolutely worst clothes, like grungy jeans with holes in the knees and dirty, torn T-shirts!

Play the air guitar

Playing *air guitar* is easy as long as you have a tape or CD of a great guitarist, like Eric Clapton or Bruce Springsteen playing in the background. What's an air guitar, you ask? Why, it's an invisible electric guitar — made of air.

To play air guitar, put on rock music, preferably a song with a great guitar solo. Then pretend to play the strings of your guitar with your left hand in front of your belly button. Hold your right hand in the the air over your right shoulder, as if you were holding a guitar.

Really *feel* the music you're listening to. Let it get inside you, and grab your guts. Be the guitar player, bending your knees, squeezing your eyes, bobbing your head around, stomping and swaying to the beat. The more you let it rip and wail, the greater your air guitar will be!

A rock group decoration

Make a rock 'n' roll group to decorate the table at your rock 'n' roll party. Collect and wash a group of rocks from outside, and then paint outrageous faces on them — as if they were rock stars in the middle of a concert. Bright-colored thread or yarn glued on for hair, and glittery make-up, add to the effect.

Set the decorated rocks on a place mat next to some rolls you got from the bakery (or baked yourself!). There you have it — rock 'n' roll!

WHO WERE THE BEATLES?

Once upon a time back in the early 1960s, four teenagers from Liverpool, England turned the whole world on its ear. They were the *Beatles* — John Lennon, Paul McCartney, George Harrison, and Ringo Starr.

The music they created was so full of life and so much fun that for one beautiful moment in history, music making became the biggest news of the day. Every night, TV news and newspaper headlines followed the doings of the "Fab Four," as they were sometimes called. Fans jammed their concerts. Girls shrieked their names. People all over the globe wore their hair with bangs, mop-top style, like the Beatles wore theirs.

History has never seen anything like it, before or since. The Beatles conquered the world and everyone in it — not with bombs and guns — but with the positive power of music.

• STYLE FESTIVAL •

Now that you're acquainted with a bunch of different musical styles, here's a "stylish" game to play by yourself, or with friends.

Write down the names of different musical styles on small pieces of paper. Write rock 'n' roll, classical, jazz, operetta, Broadway musical, blues, and any other style that comes to mind. Then put the papers in a jar or hat.

Next, choose a simple song you know and try improvising it in these different musical styles. For instance, take the song *I've Been Working on the Railroad*. Sing it as if it were a rock 'n' roll tune. Now try it as a jazz tune, Broadway musical, or an opera. Amazing how the same notes can give out so many different feelings, isn't it?

SHARING THE FUN

Now that you've got a bagful of musical skills, tricks, and things to do, it's time to get together with others to share them. Sharing is definitely one of the best things about music — the more you share the music you love, the more you get to have it in your life!

MAKE A PARADE!

Everybody loves a parade — especially when there's music in it. It's fun to march around to the beat of a drum! And all it takes is a leader, a beat, and a reason for marching.

The leader is the person who marches in front, setting the pace of the parade. The leader should have a wand or baton (the twirling kind is best) to move up and down, in time to the music.

As for the reason for your parade, well, almost any will do. A rainy-day parade around the house is as much fun as a sunny-day parade, up and down the block! Why not celebrate International Aviation Day with a homemade parade? Or make up a holiday of your own, like International Soup Day, or Kids Celebrate Today parade. Cheer up a neighbor by marching by the house with a banner saying something like, "We Love Mrs. Jones!"

The parade beat

Don't have a drum? Then get a pot from the kitchen and something soft, like a wooden spoon or homemade mallet, to bang it with. (A metal spoon would be too loud.) The basic beat should be good and booming, but with plenty of room for other instruments to be heard (see pages 68–69).

A carton parade drum

Punch holes on the side of a cardboard box. Cut out discs of cardboard to serve as "washers," and then string some yarn through the holes in the box so that the box comes to your hip. Sling the yarn over your shoulder when marching, and play with your hands or with a mallet.

Every parade needs a drum beat

The basic mood of a parade is set by the drum beat and the marching music. Try this drum beat on all kinds of drums.

1 2 **3** 1 2
1 2 **3** 1 2
1 2 **3**
1 2 **3**
1 2 **3** 1 2
(repeat)

Or, put these words to a beat for another fine parade beat:

Boom bah la

Boom bah la

Boom bah la

Boom

Ricketee

Ricketee

Rack

Rack

Kazoom!

(repeat)

Whistles, fifes, bells, and kazoos

Any hand-held instrument will add to your parade, the more the merrier. You can probably find a few around the house if you take a *Musical Safari* (see page 72).

PARADE CHANTS — SOUND OFF!

It's fun to make up a special chant to march to. Just get a couple of phrases, preferably ones that rhyme, and call them out loud and clear. You can make up chants of your own. Or try these to start with:

Aren't you tired? (boom) (boom)

Of TV! (boom) (boom)

Shut it off! (boom) (boom)

Come with me! (boom) (boom)

Or, how about:

All the kids! (boom) (boom)

On this street! (boom) (boom)

Are the best! (boom) (boom)

You will meet! (boom) (boom)

Parade songs

Marching songs add to the fun of a parade. Songs like *When the Saints Go Marching In, Yankee Doodle, Grand Old Flag,* and *Strike Up the Band* are all fun to march to. So is the Beatles' *Yellow Submarine.* A good parade technique is to keep the drum beating from one song to another with no breaks in between. The leader will call out the next song, and start you all together. If you are playing hand-held instruments, don't forget to use that other always-with-you instrument — your voice! Sing out!

When the Saints Go Marching In

This old favorite comes from New Orleans, the home of jazz:

Oh, when the saints, go marching in,

Oh, when the saints go marching in,

How I want to be in that number,

When the saints go marching in!

You can change the words to suit your parade, too. How about this one sung to the same favorite melody?

Oh, when the kids, come marching in,

Oh, when the kids come marching in,

You'd better run very fast then!

When the kids come marching in!

HAVE A HOOTENANNY!

Sing your heads off!

When people get together to open up and sing, it's a *hootenanny* — or sing-a-long. There can be two people or ten — the more the merrier! If you have a guitar or keyboard player who knows three chords, so much the better. (See Encore, page 150.) But as you've proven in this book, you don't need instruments to make music. Singing voices and clapping hands make fine orchestras, all by themselves.

Make a list

Begin by jotting a list of songs you think your family and friends will know. Ask others to help you. That list will be your guide at the sing-a-long. You may want to make copies of the words to some songs, too. Lots of times, people only remember the first line of a song.

Think about groups of songs, like railroad songs, river songs, sunshine songs, Beatles' tunes, and rounds.

Warning: Once you get started making a song list, you can be sure more and more songs will get on it! The people you invite to your hootenanny will think of a bunch of songs to sing when they get there, too! You don't have to have any special order — sing-a-longs are just for fun! Try ending your hootenanny with lullabies and goodnight songs.

Favorite sing-a-long songs

If you don't know the words and tunes of these songs, ask around. Someone you know will!

Yellow Submarine (and other Beatles' tunes)

Michael Row the Boat Ashore

Kumbaya

Green Grow the Rushes

If I Had a Hammer

Follow the Drinking Gourd

Mama Don't Allow

This Land Is Your Land

Shenandoah

Take Me Out to the Ball Game

So Long It's Been Good to Know You

Goodnight, Irene

• A VERSE AND A CHORUS •

A verse comes before the chorus. Each verse always has different words.

The chorus is the part of a song that comes after the verse and is repeated over and over again, after each verse.

For example, in the song *Oh, Susannah!*, the verse starts with, "I come from Alabama with a banjo on my knee . . . ." The chorus begins, "Oh, Susannah, oh don't you cry for me . . . ."

In *Home on the Range*, "Oh, give me a home, where the buffalo roam" begins the first verse. "Home, home on the range" is the beginning of the chorus.

Sing-a-long snacks

Singing makes people thirsty and hungry so have some snacks on hand at your hootenanny.

When you serve the snacks, ask people to sing any music they remember from commercials. Music from ads is called *jingles*, and people have fun remembering all their silly words and tunes. See if people remember which jingles go with which products. Sometimes the music has more impact than the name of the product.

Musical Circle

Musical circle is a lot like musical chairs, but it's less competitive. In musical circle, you and your friends walk in a circle until the music stops. Then you all plop down to the ground. Last one down is out, and so is anyone who sits before the music stops. Play until you have a winner. Then play again, for more fun.

HAVE A KITCHEN CABARET

A cabaret (ka-bah-RAY) is a place where music is performed, usually on a small stage, for an audience that is eating or drinking. At home, you can create the perfect cabaret right in your kitchen or dining room.

Creating the material

Making up material for a cabaret show is lots of fun because cabarets have comedy, drama, and music in them. A funny song, a love song, a comment about life, a few jokes — there's room for it all in a cabaret.

Ladies and Gentlemen, May I introduce . . . ?

Cabarets always have an *MC* — a *Master*, or *Mistress, of Ceremonies*. The MC's job is introducing the performers and calling for applause. Take turns being the MC if more than one person wants the job.

We've got a real treat for you tonight

If you plan the cabaret acts during the day, you can surprise your family at night. Suppose it's after supper, but before dessert. Hurry to clear the table, set up a tall stool for performers, if you have one (if not, have performers stand), and then ask your audience to sit down again. If they drink tea or coffee, make sure they have it for the show.

Then the MC can call for everyone's attention:

"Good evening, Ladies and Gentlemen, and you, too, Spanky. I'd like to welcome you to the Wagner Kids' Kitchen Cabaret, where we serve up the best in family entertainment. Tonight we have some very special guests, starting with a talented young lady we all know so well. She's right here by the microwave waiting to warm us all up. Come on, and say hello, Sis!"

The acts

The songs and skills you've learned — lip synching, one-kid-band with homemade instruments, doo-wop or jug band music, scat singing — even an animal trick or some knock knock jokes — are all great in a cabaret show. Anything goes as long as it displays some sort of skill.

The secret is for the MC to lead the applause after each act, saying something like, "Hey, that was great, Sis. We didn't know *Twinkle, Twinkle, Little Star* could sound so good as rock 'n' roll! Give her a big hand, ladies and gentlemen! "

At the end of the cabaret show, the MC thanks the performers and the audience, "You're beautiful, everybody, I really mean it, and wasn't that some card trick by Uncle Al?"

A family tradition

A kids' cabaret can become a unique and wonderful family tradition. It's especially fun when cousins, aunts, uncles, and grandparents come to visit. It's a great time to ask Grandma and Grandpa to sing their special song — the one that was popular when they fell in love. If you have a home video recorder, you might even want to tape the shows for posterity!

• BARBECUE JAMBOREE •

Hey, all you cowpokes, and lovers of the fabled west! You can have yourself a western jamboree — even if you live in the city or out in the 'burbs! With music, a jamboree can be as much fun in a backyard or living room as it is under the starry sky of the open range.

Serve your songs up with some baked beans, hot dogs, or soy nugget Sloppy Joes, and a mug of burnt tea. Plaid shirts, blue jeans, bandannas, and cowboy hats add to the fun.

Herding 'em up

Cowboys called the cows they were leading "little dogies." But the little dogies they were talking about were not the tame, peaceful cattle we know today. They were *longhorn cattle*, fierce animals that weighed over a thousand pounds each. These huge beasts were strong and wily, too. Their natural enemies were wolves and grizzly bears, so nature gave them horns and sharp hooves to fight with! Herding longhorn cattle wasn't easy, even for the strongest cowpuncher.

Git Along Little Dogies

This waltz (1-2-3 beat) is one of the oldest cowboy songs. It's about a cowboy herding cattle on a long trip to Wyoming. Ask a grown-up to hum you the tune, or simply clap out the waltz beat as you say the words. You'll find these words almost sing themselves.

Verse 1:

As I was a-walking one morning for pleasure,

I spied a young cowpuncher riding alone,

His hat was throwed back and his spurs was a-jingling,

As he approached me a-singing this song

Chorus:

Whoop-ee ti yi yo, git along little do-gies,

It's your misfortune and none of my own,

Whoop-ee ti yi yo, git a long little do-gies,

For you know Wyoming will be your new home.

Verse 2:

Oh, some fellas go up the trail just for pleasure,

But that's where they've got it most awfully wrong,

You haven't an idea the trouble they give us,

As we go a-drivin' them dogies along!

• SLOPPY JOES — WITHOUT THE COW •

These meatless Sloppy Joes taste as good as the original recipe.

- 2 tablespoons olive oil
- 1/2 onion, chopped in small pieces
- Minced garlic, to taste
- 1 cup soy nuggets (found in any health food store)
- 1 small can tomato paste
- 1 package Sloppy Joes seasoning
- 2 cups water

In a skillet, cook the olive oil, onions, and garlic until the onions are soft. Add the soy nuggets, tomato paste, Sloppy Joes seasoning, and water.

Stir and serve on a toasted English muffin or hamburger roll. Yum!

Make a western vest

You can make a western-style vest to wear for your jamboree. You'll need a large brown grocery bag, scissors, and markers, or crayons, to decorate.

Cut the bag up the middle and cut out a section for your neck. Cut holes for your arms. Make fringe on the bottom and decorate with fancy designs.

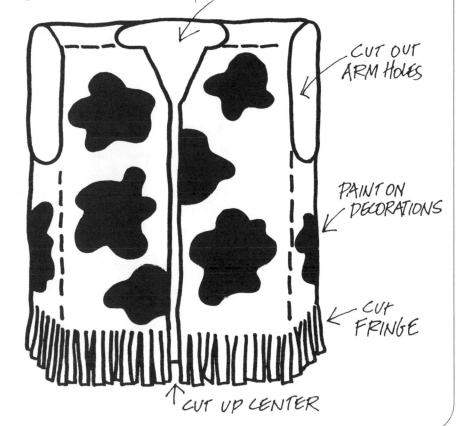

WESTERN PAPER BAG VEST

CUT OUT NECK SECTION

CUT OUT ARM HOLES

PAINT ON DECORATIONS

CUT FRINGE

CUT UP CENTER

COWBOY'S BEST FRIEND

A cowboy's life could be hard and lonely, and his horse was often his best friend. Out on the wide open prairie, driving cattle, his horse's faithfulness and intelligence helped many a cowpoke out of a jam.

In the following song, *Old Paint* is this cowboy's name for his pinto pony. Pintos are horses with different colors on their hide, that look as if they were painted. "Throwing the houlihan" is a dangerous game that's now outlawed. In it, a cowboy jumped off a running horse onto the horns of a steer, knocking him to the ground!

A "coulee" (KOO-lee) is a kind of small canyon. The "fiery and the snuffy" are longhorn cattle that want to be moving along.

Create the sound of horses' hooves

If you like the sound of horses' hooves, you can make it with your hands. The beat is a quick one, two, three. Here's how to make it:

On one: Clap hands.
On two: Let one hand slide to your thigh and slap it.
On three: The other hand slaps the other thigh.
Repeat that pattern faster and faster and you'll soon hear horses' hooves galloping right where you are!

I Ride an Old Paint

I ride an Old Paint, I lead an old Dan,
I'm going to Montana for to throw the houlihan.
They feed in the coulees, they water in the draw,
Their tails are all matted, and their backs are all raw.

> *Chorus:*
> *Git along you little dogies, git along there, slow*
> *For the fiery and the snuffy are a-raring to go!*

When I die take my saddle down from the wall,
Just saddle my pony and lead him from his stall.
Just tie on my carcass, and turn our faces west,
We'll ride on the prairies to the place we love best.

A humble home

Many of the very first settlers who lived on the prairie, or the range, as they called it, lived in sod houses. They cut a hole in the earth, and made walls from mud. For doors and windows, they used whatever they had on hand — thick blankets or rough boards. Still, though their dwellings were crude, their neighbors were friendly and helpful, and the western air was said to be so sweet and pure that just breathing it would make a sick person healthy!

Home on the Range

Oh, give me a home, where the buffalo roam,

And the deer and the antelope play.

Where seldom is heard a discouraging word,

And the skies are not cloudy all day.

Chorus:

Home, home on the range

Where the deer and the antelope play

Where seldom is heard a discouraging word,

And the skies are not cloudy all day

• A REAL RANGE •

The Nature Conservancy is an organization that buys land with endangered species on it and promises to keep that land natural forever. They bought 30,000 acres in Oklahoma that used to be a tall grass prairie, or range. Now they're turning it back to a real range, complete with antelope, buffalo, and the grasses and prairie flowers that were there before the settlers came.

You can visit the Nature Conservancy's Tall Grass Prairie Project if you go to Oklahoma. Their phone number is 612-331-0700. What a great place to sing about the Old West!

More songs for a Barbecue Jamboree

Sweet Betsy from Pike

So Long, It's Been Good to Know You

Clementine

Down in the Valley

Red River Valley

The Streets of Laredo

• A BEATNIK CAFE IN THE GARAGE •

First, a little history. Way, way back in the 1950s, maybe even before your parents were born, and even before the age of "hippies," there were *beatniks.*

What's a beatnik, you ask? A beatnik was a person who was interested in the deeper meaning of life and not very interested in money or the things money can buy. Beatniks tried hard to figure life out by writing and chanting poetry and songs.

They got together in *cafes,* or *coffeehouses,* to express themselves. There, to the pulsing rhythm of bongo drums, they would read their poetry and sing their songs.

Today, in some places, coffeehouses are coming back. It seems people are still trying to figure life out by writing poetry and making up songs!

P.S. Even though the true beatniks had little interest in money, this is one activity that you can do to raise some! Lots of grown-ups might be willing to pay a small entrance fee for the chance to go back in time at your cafe.

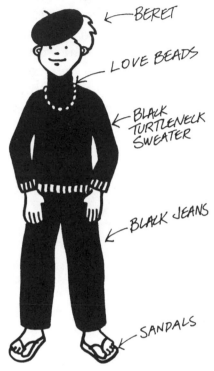

BERET

LOVE BEADS

BLACK TURTLENECK SWEATER

BLACK JEANS

SANDALS

Dress like a beatnik

Being serious, beatniks often dressed in black, especially black turtleneck sweaters and black jeans. Being simple in their taste, they often wore sandals on their feet, or berets on their heads. Some, male and female, wore native seed necklaces, later called "Love Beads." Male beatniks often wore beards.

Peanut shells on the floor

Beatnik cafes were not very fancy places. Anyone, even people without much money, could go to the cafe and sit for hours, drinking espresso coffee and listening to poetry. Your garage is the perfect place to set up your cafe. A card table or turned over carton with a pillow-case tablecloth and some folding chairs are all you need to furnish your cafe.

If you have a tape recorder, try to find some cool jazz music, like Dave Brubeck's *Take Five* or an old Stan Getz recording to play in the background. Hot cider makes a good beatnik drink, especially when it's served in old mugs that don't match. If you promise to clean up, put bowls of unshelled peanuts on the cafe tables so the cafe guests can munch, as they listen and think.

Poetry and bongo drums

Beatnik poetry is very intense — even when it's funny. To try writing some of your own, ask yourself a serious question, like, "What is the meaning of life?" You can answer seriously or with your tongue-in-your-cheek, which means in a joking manner. We promise that the poem you create on that theme will be a perfect beatnik poem, no matter how it turns out.

If you want to read some authentic beatnik poetry, look for books by Lawrence Ferlinghetti or Allen Ginsberg from the library. Have some poems and books available for others to read from, if the moment strikes them right.

Ask a friend to drum while you chant or sing your poem at the cafe. There's no need to rehearse this act. Just let the moment take you.

• MOUNTAIN MUSIC! MAKE A JUG BAND •

Got some whistles, bottles, bells, and things to bang on? Yee-haw! Then you're all set and ready to create a jug band. All you need are some homemade instruments, a few simple songs, and the vim and vigor to put them across.

Jug band music is good in the kitchen or out in the yard. Play for family, friends, or just for fun. Or, have a jug band picnic or birthday party where people dress country-style and bring their own home-made instruments!

Nothing fancy

Jug bands first started in America's Appalachian Mountains, where people loved music but often lacked money for instruments or music lessons. They did what you can do; they put together a collection of found instruments and played their music just for fun. (See page 60.)

People enjoyed hearing this music so much that word started getting around. Soon, jug bands became popular all over the country.

← STRAW HAT

← BANDANNA

← PLAID SHIRT

← OVERALLS

← ARMY BOOTS

Jug band costumes

It's fun to dress up like traditional mountain folk for a jug band. Costumes made of blue jeans, bandannas, plaid shirts, and overalls are perfect for performing mountain music. So are straw hats, flowery print dresses, and army boots. Try on some of a grown-up's old clothes for fun. An eyebrow pencil is good for make-believe freckles, too.

Performing with your jug band

Of course, you don't have to perform for other people. Jug band music is fun all by itself. But you add to the fun when you share your music with others. Even little kids enjoy being in a jug band show. Once you get some experience, you can even find a senior citizen center or hospital that would enjoy a short jug band program.

← STRAW HAT

← FRECKLES

← BRAIDS WITH BOWS

← PRINT DRESS

← ARMY BOOTS

• PUTTIN' ON THE SHINE •

Any country-style name is good for your jug band. You can call yourselves by your family name, as in, The Johnson Family Singers. Or, if you live near a mountain range, think about borrowing its name for your band. The Watchung Wailers, Jenny Jump Jug Band, and Ozark Orchestra are all names that come from mountain ranges.

When you're putting together your band, it's okay to call each other affectionate names like Mammy, Pappy, Billy Bob, or Lil' Suzy Q. How about calling the youngest member of the group Granpaw, or Grammaw?

Yuk it up!

In between songs, throw in a few jokes, the cornier the better. You can punctuate the punch line with a bang on a pot. For instance, suppose you and Auntie Myrtle are in front of an audience. Suzy can say, "Aunt Myrtle, your coffee — it always tastes like mud!"

To which Auntie can answer: "Well, I should hope so! I make fresh ground!" (clang)

That one didn't grab you? How about this one:

Grampaw says: "Suzy, show the people how smart you are. Spell the word rain."

Suzy answers: "Why that's easy! Rain is spelled, R-A-N-E."

"Why, Suzy," says Grampaw, shaking his head, "That's the worst spell of rain we've had here in a long time!"

A MOUNTAIN MUSIC PROGRAM

Here's a sample jug band program made up of songs that are easy to sing and play. Keep time by stomping your feet, slapping your knees, or clapping to the beat.

She'll Be Coming 'Round the Mountain

Old MacDonald Had a Farm

Sweet Betsy from Pike

On Top of Spaghetti

Here's an old favorite sung to the tune of *On Top of Old Smokey*. It's a sad tale about a bouncing meat-ball, sung to a waltz (1-2-3) rhythm.

*On top of spaghetti
All covered with cheese,
I lost my poor meatball
When somebody sneezed*

*It rolled off the table
And onto the floor,
And then my poor meatball
Rolled right out the door*

*It rolled in the garden
And under a bush,
And then my poor meatball
Was nothing but mush.*

*And early next summer
It grew into a tree,
All covered with meatballs
Too yucky to eat.*

*So if you like spaghetti
All covered with cheese,
Hold onto your meatball
Should somebody sneeze!*

She'll Be Coming 'Round the Mountain

This mountain favorite has been sung for over a hundred years! Sing it in a lively, 1-2 beat. Clap as you sing and get your audience to clap and sing with you.

She'll be coming 'round the mountain when she comes
(echo: when she comes!)
She'll be coming 'round the mountain when she comes
(echo: when she comes)
She'll be coming 'round the mountain,
She'll be coming 'round the mountain,
She'll be coming 'round the mountain when she comes!

More verses:

She'll be riding six white horses when she comes
(echo: whoa there!)
Oh, we'll all go down to meet her when she comes
(echo: Hi, babe!)
She'll be wearing red pajamas when she comes
(echo: scratch, scratch)
Oh, she'll have to sleep with Gramma when she comes
(echo: snore, snore)
We'll eat french fries with gravy when she comes
(echo: yum, yum)
Oh, we'll all be sad and lonely when she goes
(echo: boo hoo)

For extra fun, try this: In between verses, say the echoes in the order they came in, "whoa there; Hi, babe!; scratch, scratch; snore, snore; yum, yum; boo hoo." Then try adding hand motions to match the words, such as patting your tummy for "yum, yum."

• A MUSICAL MULTICULTURAL PARTY •

One big family

There's an old saying that says "everyone's a little Jewish." Well, the same goes for everyone being a little Italian, German, English, Chinese, Russian, African, Korean, Hungarian, Greek, Irish, and Indian. Make that Polish, Dutch, Japanese, and every other kind of people, too.

According to math experts, everyone on earth is related to everyone else by being at least his thirty-second cousin! Yes, the human race is one, big, enormous, gigantic, tremendous, huge family! So when we celebrate someone else's heritage, we're really celebrating a little part of our own, too!

Have a multicultural party

When people from many different backgrounds and cultures respect each other's differences, learn about each other's traditions, and all get along, that's called *multiculturalism*. You can have a multicultural party with music and dancing from all over the world! It's like creating the United Nations in your own home! Ask your friends and neighbors to bring their favorite recordings of music from their "home country." And be sure to ask them to dress in traditional costumes, if they want to. Lastly, but very importantly, ask them to bring a pot-luck dish of a traditional food from the country they want to represent.

• A MUSICAL JAPANESE TEA CEREMONY •

In Japan, serving and drinking tea is a very special activity, especially when music is played. But you don't have to go to Tokyo to have a *Japanese tea ceremony*. You can have one right in your own home.

All you need is a low table to serve the tea on. (If you don't have one, ask a grown-up to help you cut down a large cardboard box to use as a tea table.) You won't need chairs, because in traditional Japanese houses, people sit on pillows, or rest on their knees for tea.

When you bring the tea to the table, put it down and bow to your guests, from the waist. Call the person you are serving by his or her name, followed by the word *san*. That's a term of respect and endearment in Japanese. "This is for you, Mary-san. Enjoy your tea, Michael-san."

Music for the ceremony

Here is a beautiful Japanese song from the Aizu district, a place of great beauty with lovely lakes, mountains, and valleys. The melody is delicate and lilting. After you bring the tea, you can sing or hum this song while the tea brews.

We have written the melody with smiley faces to show you where the tune goes go up or down. It's okay if you don't read music — just feel for the melody by going up and down like the notes do, humming what you think they might be. It will sound beautiful if you hum softly and smile, too.

The melody is written in 1-2-3-4 time, counted here as 1 & 2 & 3 & 4 &. Some of the smiley faces are "holding hands" with a neighboring face. These share a 1 &; all other faces get the full 1 & beat to themselves.

Aizu Melody

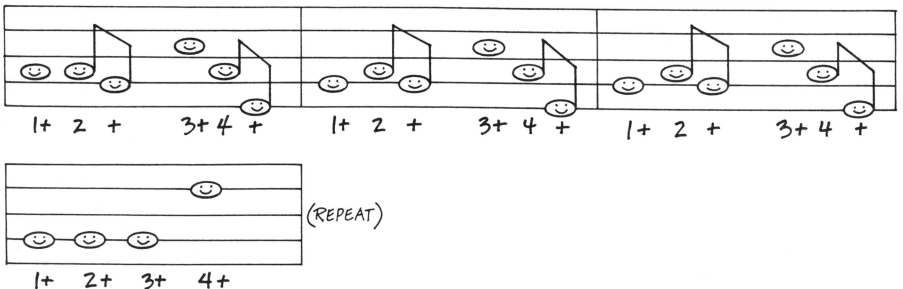

A rubber band lute made from an empty tissue box has a delicate Asian sound that is perfect for the tea ceremony (see page 64).

A tea ceremony costume

In Japan, people wear loose fitting clothing called *kimonos* when they have a tea ceremony. In place of a *kimono*, wear a bathrobe with a wide sash, tied in the back.

Wear slippers or sandals on your feet. Japanese people traditionally do not wear shoes in their homes.

Tea ceremony snacks

Rice cakes, especially the small-sized ones, are the perfect food at a tea ceremony. Sprinkle thinly sliced or grated apples and cinnamon on top for a yummy treat.

• CELEBRATE RUSSIA WITH A TROIKA •

Russia is a big country where the weather can be very cold. In the old days, horses pulled sleds over long distances. A *troika* is a sled pulled by three horses, and it is also a famous piece of music, known for its dance.

In this dance, you and your pals get to be horses! You can find the music for the troika at your library, probably in a folk music collection. (You've probably already heard it somewhere. It's a lively tune with people shouting, "Hey! Hey!")

Dance the troika!

To start the dance, the three horses line up next to one another. Let's call them Horse A, B, and C. Begin clapping out a strong, spirited **1**, 2, 3, 4 beat.

For the first 16 beats, the horses hold hands high, and prance forward 8 steps and backward 8 steps. (Prance with knees up high.)

For the next 8 beats, horses A and B form an arch for Horse C to run under. C runs under A's and B's arms, pulling B with her and running back to her original place, while A steps in place in time to the music.

That action is repeated in the next 8 beats with A going under B's and C's hand-held arch.

Next, the three horses hold hands and run to the left for 12 beats. (Hint: The dance is even more fun if you pretend to be pulling one another along.)

Then they stamp their feet hard 3 times and pause before they run to the right for 12 beats.

After that stamp 3 times, and form a straight line so you're ready to begin the dance again! Hey!

TARANTELLA FROM ITALY

Tarantella is the Italian word for spider. Inspired by the way spiders move, Italian people created a folk dance that's known the world over! Make some tambourines to dance to this lively tune. If you don't know the tune, ask around, or get it from the library.

The basic step

The basic tarantella step is very easy! Try it and you'll be sure to succeed.
Step onto your right foot and hop.
Next, step onto your left foot and hop.
Step, hop, step, hop. Got it? Good!

Now, as you step and hop on your right foot, swing the left out and across it, and do the same with your right foot when you hop left.

Honestly, it's much harder to write about the tarantella than it is to dance it!

While your feet are step-hop-swinging, keep your upper body straight and proud, with one hand at your hip, and the other in the air. Shake and bang your tambourine (see page 70) in time to the music!

The dance

Start by making a circle, and face the center. For 8 beats, step-hop to the right, and for 8 beats, to the left.

Then, put your hands behind you and take small skipping steps forward to the center of the circle while gradually bringing your hands up. Give the tambourine a good bang, or clap your hands loudly at the center.

Then, step back and give another bang when you reach the outer circle, and do the dance again!

MEXICAN HAT DANCE

If you can find an old sombrero, put it in the center of the circle while you do this folk dance. Ask a grown-up to hum the tune for you. If he or she isn't sure whether they know it, try sharing this code with them. It just might jog their memory:

Da DUM Da DUM Da DUM! CLAP-CLAP!
Da deedle dee dum da dum! CLAP-CLAP!
Da DUM Da DUM Da DUM! CLAP-CLAP!
Da deedle dee dum da dum!

The basic step

In one hopping movement, bring your right leg back as your left goes forward, with the left heel in and down, and the left toe up and out. Switch your feet, left and right, until you get the feel of it. For the dance, you'll do three of these steps, and then clap two times quickly.

When the music changes, it's time to go around and around and around. Do this by spinning in place, first one way, then the other. In the next to last measure of the song, get down on your right knee, raise your hands, and shout, "Hey!"

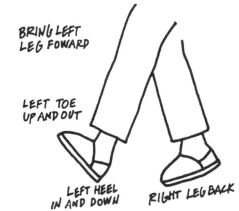

BRING LEFT LEG FOWARD

LEFT TOE UP AND OUT

LEFT HEEL IN AND DOWN   RIGHT LEG BACK

SWITCH FEET AND REPEAT

SWITCH FEET AND REPEAT

• THE ISRAELI HORA •

In Israel, the national dance is the *hora*. But this dance is so much fun and so easy to learn that it has become an international dance. People all over the world now use it to celebrate the happy events of their lives, especially weddings.

The hora is a circle dance. In fact, the Hebrew word *hora*, means circle. *Hava Nagila* is the song that the hora is most often danced to. *Hava nagila* is Hebrew for "Let's be happy." You can get a recording of this song from your library.

The hora

Start by forming a circle with arms out to the side so that everyone is holding each other's elbows or shoulders. Then everybody sways to the left and right. When the steps begin, start slow, and gradually pick up speed until you're dancing very fast. But don't break the circle!

In the middle of the song, all dance to the center and raise hands high. Then step back to the circle and continue dancing.

STEP LEFT WITH LEFT FOOT

CROSS RIGHT FOOT IN BACK OF LEFT

STEP LEFT, LIFT RIGHT

HOP ON LEFT, LIFT RIGHT KNEE

HOP ON RIGHT, LIFT LEFT KNEE

WALK 3 QUICK STEPS

Hora steps

Step left with left foot
Cross right foot in back of left
Step left, lift right
Hop on left, lifting right knee
Hop on right, lifting left knee
Walk quick three steps and repeat whole dance

When the music breaks on "U-ru," join hands and dance to the center with raised arms and share a group shout! Then, move back to the circle and continue the dance.

HAVE A BRAZILIAN CARNIVAL!

Every year in Brazil there's a giant dancing festival for the whole country, called Carnival. For three days and three nights, everyone dances — grandparents, parents, and kids! They all take to the streets as musicians drum out and play *samba*, *rhumba*, and *bossanova* beats for dancing.

Many of the dancers carry their own small drums, too, so they can add to the beat. Carnival dancing is free-form and easy.

Sometimes the dancers form *conga lines*, with people putting their hands on the waist of the person in front of them while they dance. The whole line dances around, weaving back and forth like a snake to the music, as people stick out their hips to one side and then the other. Conga lines are a lot of fun, and the crazier you get while doing them, like letting out some whoops and shouts, the better!

Carnival costumes

Brazilian carnival costumes are as colorful and brilliant as can be. Girls wear swirly, colorful skirts, with flowers and fruit festooned in their hair. Boys wear bright colors, too, and straw hats.

You cannot wear too much make-up at a carnival. Even men wear it in Brazil at carnival time.

Carnival flowers

Make flowers to stick behind your ears from crepe paper and wire twists. Gather the crepe paper in a bunch and twist tie it in the center. If you don't have crepe paper, use a tissue. Cut the corners off the tissue so that it is shaped like a circle. Then pick it up from the center to form the base of the flower. Attach with bobby pins.

GATHER IN CENTER WITH A TWIST TIE

CUT OFF CORNERS

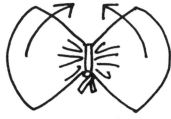

PULL UP PETALS FROM THE CENTER

ATTACH A BOBBY PIN

The Brazilian samba!

Want to get fancy with your hand-held, homemade drum? Try this Brazilian beat, called the *Samba*.

1 - 2 - 3 & 4 & 5 & 6 & 7 & 8 &

IN NIGERIA, THEY LOVE SATURDAY NIGHT — JUST LIKE WE DO!

In Nigeria, Africa, a popular song for dancing and singing is *Everybody Loves Saturday Night*. One reason why people sing it is that there's room in the words for people to throw in their own funny comments.

To dance Nigerian-style, you dance freely, bending your knees and letting your shoulders and head bob to the beat. It's a lot like the way people dance to rock 'n' roll in America! But in Nigeria, this free-style of singing and dancing is called the *High Life*!

Everybody Loves Saturday Night

Make up your own extra verses as you do the High Life! Here are some suggestions to get you started.

Everybody loves Saturday night!

Everybody loves Saturday night!

Mommy loves it! Daddy loves it! Linda loves it! I love it!

Everybody loves Saturday night!

Everybody loves shaking their hips!

Everybody loves shaking their hips!

Gramma loves it! Grampa loves it! Baby loves it! I love it!

Everybody loves shaking their hips!

And more . . . .

There are so many wonderful dances and kinds of traditional music the world over. Perhaps someone at your multicultural party will know how to do the Irish Jig, the Greek Misalou, or traditional dances from Scotland, Sweden, or Asia, too.

Here are the lyrics to a song we wrote just for all of you. It expresses our feelings about music and where it comes from. We hope you like it. Try making up a tune to it. Enjoy!

The Greatest Treasure Ever

The greatest treasure ever is the treasure in your mind,
Anytime you need it, it's there for you to find,
You cannot ever lose it, it'll never go away,
You can call upon it anytime, you can use it every day.

♥

You can't hold it in your hand, 'cause it lives inside of you,
It's never lost, it's with you all the time,
It's dreams, imagination, it's hope and fantasy,
The gift that's always there for you to find,
Is the treasure in your mind.

♥

The greatest treasure ever is the one inside of you,
It can take you anywhere, there's nothing it can't do,
It can open any doors for you, and take you anywhere,
You can give it all to others, and still have lots to share,

♥

You can't hold it in your hand, 'cause it lives inside of you,
It's never lost, it's with you all the time,
It's silent and invisible, fantabulous and fine,
The treasure you can never leave behind,
Is the treasure in your mind.

GOING FURTHER

If you want to explore music some more, great! One way to begin is by getting a hand-held instrument, like a *recorder* or *harmonica*. They don't cost much, but they sound great.

If you have a chance to play another instrument, lucky you! Learning to play an instrument is worth the work. Once you can play, you'll have the gift of music for your whole life!

Be sure to choose a teacher you really like, one who makes learning fun — then, never stop playing!

MUSICAL SECRETS FOR INSTRUMENT PLAYERS

Anyone who takes on the challenge of learning an instrument deserves to know these musical secrets!

Secret Number One — Don't Peek!

Magicians say the hand is quicker than the eye, and it's true! *When you play an instrument, let your hands do the work — not your eyes.* We know that it's tempting to look at the keys or the strings, but trust us on this — peeking only slows you down in the end. Leave the music making to your brain, and your fingers, and you'll learn more, faster. (How about wearing a blindfold when you practice? That's one way to avoid starting a bad habit!)

Secret Number Two: Practice Can Be Fun

It's a well-kept secret that practice can be fun when you take a creative approach. Choose a regular time of day to practice — the best time *for you*. Go over stuff you already know before you tackle new material. And be sure to save some time for cutting up, and improvising, too. You might make some cool discoveries!

If you get stuck, try pretending that you're a great musical genius who's been reborn into a clumsy body and forced to learn again, from scratch. How would Mozart deal with sausage fingers if he were starting guitar? He'd have to start slowly and practice, just like you do!

But the most important advice is this: *give yourself lots of praise* while you're practicing. Tell yourself, "I can do this!" "Hey, that was great!" and even, "This isn't easy, but I'm working at it." Keep those compliments coming — inside your head, and you'll go far!

A SUPER SECRET FOR PIANO OR GUITAR PLAYERS

Three-chord magic

A *chord* is three notes that go together, and believe it or not, learning just three chords will give you the power to play a ton of tunes!

Start by learning these chords: C, G, and F (which are in the key of C). Once you can play them well enough to change from one to the other, you're ready for three-chord magic! Here's how it works:

1. Find the note C on your instrument and sing it, as if it were the last note of the song you want to play. *The last note of a song almost always tells the key the song is written in, and you need songs in the key of C.*

2. Now, start the song from the beginning, playing on the C chord. It will sound fine for a while, but then it won't fit anymore. That means it's time to change chords, to either G or F. Keep going through the song. After some trial and error, you'll begin to get a feel for when to switch to C, G, or F. Keep at it and soon this will all come naturally — we promise!

Three-chord magic song list

Here are just a few of the songs you can play on three chords:

Bingo, Old MacDonald, Jimmy Crack Corn, I've Been Working on the Railroad, Michael Row the Boat Ashore, You Take the High Road, Happy Birthday, Yellow Submarine, Twist and Shout, Amazing Grace, She'll Be Coming 'Round the Mountain, When the Saints Go Marching In, Down by the Riverside, Silent Night, On Top of Spaghetti — and about a million more!

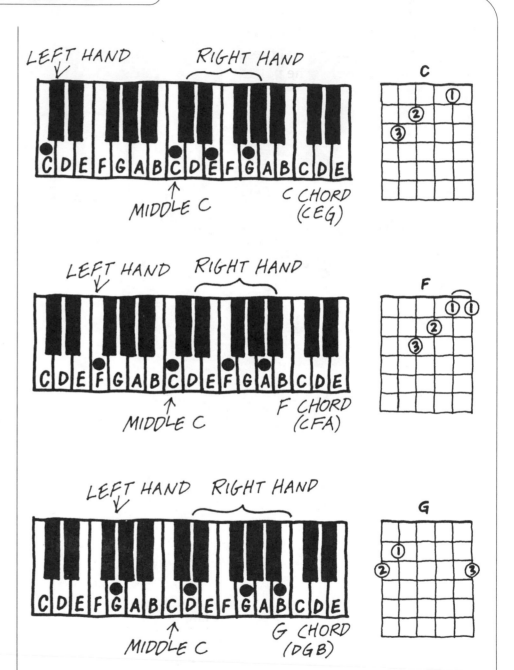

Twelve-bar blues with three-chord magic

You can create and play real twelve-bar blues songs on just three chords, too. Here's the pattern:

Play C for 16 beats,
F for 8 beats,
C for 8 beats,
G for 4 beats,
F for 4 beats,
C for 4 beats,
G for 4 beats.

Try it and see how easy blues can be!

FOR GUITAR PLAYERS ONLY: AN OPEN SECRET

This secret will give you musical powers far above your current skill level. It's called *open tuning*. Open tuning is a way of tuning the guitar so that however you strum on the strings, you make a musical sound. In fact, *anyone who picks up an open-tuned guitar and strums it will sound good!*

The secret is that the six strings are tuned so that they all go together like one big chord. Don't think of it as cheating, either. It's just another way to play. (Music great Richie Havens built his whole career on open tuning.)

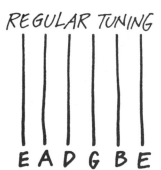

OPEN TUNING

D A D G A D

REGULAR TUNING

E A D G B E

Tuning to an open chord

To take advantage of open tuning, you'll need to re-tune three strings, by bringing them down one whole note. Change the first (fattest) string from F to D; the fifth string from B to A, and the sixth (narrowest) from E to D. That's all there is to it.

Now pick up the guitar and strum. Suddenly, you're making beautiful music!

To play a chord, put four flattened fingers right behind, but not on, the fret (those little slats on the neck of the guitar) you're playing. Move your hand up and down the neck to change chords.

It's that simple. Open tuning works. (It also works on any stringed instrument! So if you find Grandpa's old violin up in the attic, open tune it, get out your bow, and flail away!)

Three-chord magic on an open-tuned guitar

Make three-chord magic on an open-tuned guitar by playing with the D, G, and A chords. For D, strum the guitar without holding any strings down. For A, press your hand across the fifth fret, and for G, press it against the seventh fret chord. Presto! You can now play a thousand tunes!

5TH FRET
PRESS ACROSS STRINGS TO MAKE "G" CHORD

7TH FRET
PRESS ACROSS STRINGS TO MAKE "A" CHORD

1ST 2ND 3RD 4TH 5TH 6TH 7TH 8TH 9TH 10TH ETC.

DON'T WORRY THESE ARE JUST FRETS

D–G–A IS A MAGIC 3 CHORD COMBO

FOR INSTANT KEYBOARD MAGIC — PLAY THE BLACK KEYS

Sit at any keyboard and play the black keys — just the black ones. The black keys are mysterious, magical, and enchanting. You can make a whole concert on them.

Let your imagination lead you when you play. Can you make the sound of water, rippling in a mountain stream? Pretend you are playing in a forest, and let the black keys imitate the woodland sounds around you. Or pretend you are wearing a tuxedo, playing in a big concert hall. The key is to create a direct line between your imagination and your fingers — and something about the black keys makes imaginations fly!

Songs for black keys alone

You can also play several songs just by using the black keys. Try these and see how easy piano-playing can be.

The Farmer in the Dell (The = C#, Farm = F#)

Old Dan Tucker (starts on Bb)

Cindy (I = C#, Wish = D#)

Old MacDonald Had a Farm (starts on F#)

Auld Lang Syne (Should = C# Auld = F#)

Swing Low, Sweet Chariot (starts on Bb)

Goodbye Old Paint (Eb, Db)

READING, WRITING, AND RHYTHMATIC: A CRASH COURSE ON ONE PAGE

Read music — with your hands!

You can learn to read music just by looking at your hands. We'll prove it:

Here is a music staff, with five lines, and four spaces between them.

Here is a hand. It has five fingers, and four spaces between them.

Here's how they connect!

Name the notes on the lines: E - G - B - D - F (memory clue: Every Good Boy Does Fine)

Name the notes on the spaces: F-A-C-E

Reading rhythm

Say this out loud:

WHOLE: Say it slow and clap 4 times. A whole note takes, 4 beats.

SPILL: Say it slow and count to 2. That's a half note, 2 beats.

CUP: Say it on the count of 1. It's a quarter note, 1 beat.

PEP-PER: Say it quickly. Those are eighth notes, or half beats.

MER-RI-LY: You've just said triplets, three notes in one beat.

GOTTA GOTTA: Say it in one beat and you've said sixteenth notes. They go really fast!

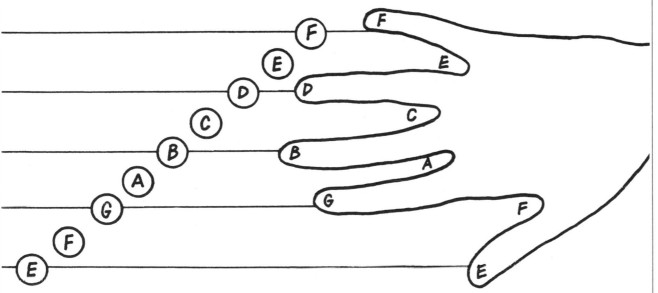

MORE KiDS CAN! BOOKS FROM WiLLiAMSON PUBLiSHiNG

To order additional copies of **KIDS MAKE MUSIC!**, please enclose $12.95 per copy plus $2.50 shipping and handling. Follow "To Order" instructions on the last page. Thank you.

KIDS & WEEKENDS!
Creative Ways to Make Special Days
by Avery Hart and Paul Mantell

Packed with truly creative ways to play, have fun, learn, grow, and build self-esteem and positive relationships, this book is a must for every parent, grandparent, baby-sitter, and teacher. Hart and Mantell will inspire us all to transform some part of every weekend — even if it is only 30 minutes — into a special experience. Everything from backyard nature to putting on a magic show to creating a bird sanctuary to writing a book about yourself to environmentally sound activities indoors and out. Whatever your interests, no matter how busy you are, kids and their families will savor special weekend moments.

176 pages, 11 x 8^1/$_2$, over 400 illustrations
Quality paperback, $12.95

THE KIDS' MULTICULTURAL ART BOOK
Arts & Craft Experiences from Around the World
by Alexandra M. Terzian

Children will reach across continents and oceans with paper, paste, and paints, while absorbing basic sensibilities about the wondrous cultures of others. Children will learn by making such things as the *Korhogo Mud Cloth* and the *Wodaabe Mirror Pouch* from Africa, the *Chippawa Dream Catcher* of the American Indian, the *Kokeshi Doll* of Japan, *Chinese Egg Painting*, the Mexican *Folk Art Tree of Life*, the *Twirling Palm Puppet* from India, and the Guatemalan *Green Toad Bank*. A virtual feast of multicultural art and craft experiences!

160 pages, 11 x 8^1/$_2$, over 400 how-to-do-it illustrations
Quality paperback, $12.95

EcoArt!
Earth-Friendly Art & Craft Experiences for 3- to 9-year-olds
by Laurie Carlson

What better way to learn to love and care for the Earth than through creative art play! Laurie Carlson's latest book is packed with 150 projects using only recyclable, reusable, or nature's own found art materials. These fabulous activities are sure to please any child!

160 pages, 11 x 8$^{1}/_{2}$, 400 illustrations
Quality paperback, $12.95

KIDS COOK!
Fabulous Food for the Whole Family
by Sarah Williamson and Zachary Williamson

Here's a cookbook written for kids by two teenagers who know what kids like to eat! *Kids Cook!* is filled with over 150 recipes for great tasting foods that kids ages 8 and up can cook for themselves and for their families and friends, too. Try breakfast bananzas like *Breakfast Sundaes*, great lunches including *Chicken Shirt Pocket*, super salads like *A Whale of a Fruit Salad*, quick snacks and easy extras like *Nacho Nibbles*, delicious dinners including *Pizza Originale*, and dynamite desserts and soda fountain treats including *Chocolate Surprise Cupcakes*. All recipes are for "real," healthy foods — not cutesy recipes that are no fun to eat. Plus Nutri Notes, Safety First, and plenty of special menus for Father's Day, Grandma's Teatime, picnics, and parties. One terrific book!

176 pages, 11 x 8$^{1}/_{2}$, over 150 recipes, illustrations
Quality paperback, $12.95

HANDS AROUND THE WORLD
365 Creative Ways to Build Cultural Awareness & Global Respect
by Susan Milord

The latest book by award-winning author Susan Milord invites children to experience, taste, and embrace the daily lives of children from the far corners of the earth. In 365 days of experiences, it tears down stereotypes and replaces them with the fascinating realities of our differences and our similarities. Children everywhere can plant and grow, write and tell stories, draw and craft, cook and eat, sing and dance, look and explore, as they learn to live in an atmosphere of global respect and cultural awareness that is born of personal experience.

160 pages, 11 x 8$^{1}/_{2}$, over 400 illustrations
Quality paperback, $12.95

THE KIDS' NATURE BOOK
365 Indoor/Outdoor Activities and Experiences
by Susan Milord

Winner of the Parents' Choice Gold Award for learning and doing books, *The Kids' Nature Book* is loved by children, grandparents, and friends alike. Simple projects and activities emphasize fun while quietly reinforcing the wonder of the world we all share. Packed with facts and fun!

160 pages, 11 x 8$^1/_2$, 425 illustrations
Quality paperback, $12.95

ADVENTURES IN ART
Art & Craft Experiences for 7- to 14-year-olds
By Susan Milord

Imagine an art book that encourages children to explore, to experience, to touch and to see, to learn and to create . . . imagine a true adventure in art. Here's a book that teaches artisans' skills without stifling creativity. Covers making handmade papers, puppets, masks, paper seascapes, seed art, tin can lantern, berry ink, still life, silk screen, batiking, carving, and so much more. Perfect for the older child. Let the adventure begin!

160 pages, 11 x 8$^1/_2$, 500 illustrations
Quality paperback, $12.95

KIDS CREATE!
Art & Craft Experiences for 3- to 9-year-olds
by Laurie Carlson

What's the most important experience for children ages 3 to 9? Why, to create something by themselves. Carlson provides over 150 creative experiences ranging from making dinosaur sculptures to clay cactus gardens, from butterfly puppets to windsocks. Plenty of help for the parents working with the kids, too! A delightfully innovative book.

160 pages, 11 x 8$^1/_2$, over 400 illustrations
Quality paperback, $12.95

KIDS LEARN AMERICA!
Bringing Geography to Life with People, Places, & History
by Patricia Gordon and Reed C. Snow

Designed to help increase "geo-literacy," *Kids Learn America!* is not about memorizing. This creative and exciting new book is about making every region of our country come alive from within, about being connected to the earth and the people across this great expanse called America.• Activities and games targeted to the 50 states plus D.C. and Puerto Rico • The environment and natural resources • Geographic comparisons • Fascinating facts, famous people and places of each region. Let us all join together — kids, parents, friends, teachers, grandparents — and put America, its geography, its history, and its heritage back on the map!

176 pages, 11 x 8$^1/_2$, maps, illustrations
Trade paper, $12.95

To Order:

At your bookstore or order directly from Williamson Publishing. We accept Visa and MasterCard (please include number and expiration date), or send check to:

Williamson Publishing Company
Church Hill Road, P.O. Box 185
Charlotte, Vermont 05445

Toll-free phone orders with credit cards:
1-800-234-8791

Please add $2.50 for postage and handling. Satisfaction is guaranteed or full refund without questions or quibbles.

Please note: Prices may be slightly higher in Canada.